D1085077

*P*EERVENTION:

Training Peer Facilitators for Prevention Education

by

Robert D. Myrick, Ph.D.
and
Betsy E. Folk, Ed.D.

Student Handbook

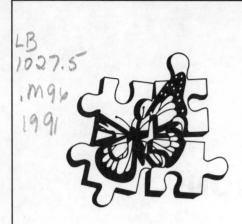

Copyright 1991
Educational Media Corporation®

Library of Congress
Catalog Card No. 90-086235

ISBN 0-932796-35-4

Printing (last Digit)

9   8   7   6   5   4   3   2   1

Publisher—

Box 21311
Minneapolis, MN 55421-0311

(612) 781-0088

Production editor—
Don L. Sorenson

Graphic design—
Earl Sorenson

Illustrator—
Paula Swenson

Dedication

To

Linda and Kaylen Myrick

and

Jay, Amber, and Shawn Folk

Betty and Vince Evans

For their love and timely support

About the Authors

Robert D. Myrick, Ph.D. is professor, Counselor Education Department, College of Education, University of Florida, Gainesville, Florida.

Betsy E. Folk, Ed.D. is Director of Admissions and Counseling, Lake Highland Preparatory School, Orlando, Florida.

Table of Contents

Robert D. Myrick and Betsy E. Folk

Chapter 1

The Need for Peer Facilitators

When Derrick arrived at Westside High School in the middle of his tenth grade year, it was his third school in two years. "My parents move a lot," he said, "and, I'm always behind in my school work. I just get settled and we move. Then, I have to start all over again. I'm not sure it's worth it." He thinks about dropping out of school. He does not want to go through the confusion and awkwardness of adjusting to a new school and unfamiliar classmates. Derrick needs help.

Sally is a good student in the middle school, but she is shy. She withdraws to herself at lunch and seldom talks with other students, who see her as bright but a little strange. "Perhaps I was too protective of her when she was younger," reports her mother, who hopes that Sally will make new friends and "get out of her cocoon." Sally's lack of self-confidence with her peers keeps her from participating in class and from taking part in school activities. Sally needs help.

At nine years of age, Jason already sees himself as an outsider. He is the smallest boy in his class and not well coordinated. He is almost always the last one chosen when teams are picked. His red hair and freckles wave a red flag for bullies, who find him an easy target for daily teasing. Jason has learned one way to get by. He has become the class clown, a regular irritant to his teacher, an annoyance to his classmates, and a puzzle to his school counselor. Jason needs help.

Who can help these students? And, who can help others like them? Young people at all grade levels have problems which range from being rejected to managing stressful busy lives. There are many students who could use help. They may have:

- poor relationships with their teachers;
- been rejected by classmates;
- problems living with their parents;
- experienced a family change, perhaps through death or divorce;
- fallen behind in their studies and are overwhelmed trying to catch up;
- no future plans and they avoid taking responsibility for what may come;
- been pressured by peers into doing illegal activities;
- eating disorders because of stress;
- problems making and keeping friends;
- test anxiety and perform poorly on class exams;
- no idea with whom they can talk about their interests, concerns, and problems; or
- poor self-concepts.

It is not easy for students to do all the things that are expected of them in school today. Expectations are higher than ever before, as schools strive to demonstrate excellence in academics, sports, music, speech, theater, the arts, and many other things. There are more choices for students, including academic and social ones.

One middle school study showed that less than a third of the student body thought there was someone in school to whom they could talk about their problems. Less than a third believed there was a teacher or friendly adult available to hear them out. Most agreed that when problems or concerns arose, the best place to find help was from another student.

Robert D. Myrick and Betsy E. Folk

The Peer Facilitator Movement

It was during the 1970s that one of the most important educational developments in our country took place. It was not a piece of fcderal or state legislation. It was not a political or social demonstration. It was neither a scientific breakthrough in teaching methods nor the restructuring of schools. It was not the coming of computers. Rather, it was a movement that took place in schools across the nation where students were systematically helping other students. Students were being organized and trained to be of assistance to others.

Education has long been valued in the Unites States. But, the demands on teachers, principals, and counselors have grown so much over the years that quality teaching time and counseling services have been squeezed out.

Too many students feel alienated from school and their teachers. Some are being pushed to the brink of frustration, maddening stress, and personal conflicts with teachers and classmates. Unfortunately, student problems have continued to mount as adult resources have appeared to dwindle. Classes are larger now than in previous years. Teachers are responsible for too many students, especially in middle and high schools.

Counselor-student ratios are too high at all grade levels in most schools (sometimes as much as 500:1), making counselors available only in crisis situations. Those students who have the most noticeable problems tend to receive help, while others are forced to work through things for themselves. Too many counselors, or other specialists, feel trapped under a deluge of paper work and non-counseling related tasks. It is often only the most assertive students that work their way through the office hurdles to reach a counselor for assistance. Even then, a majority of students know very little about the work of counselors, school psychologists, social workers, and other helping specialists and hesitate to seek their help.

There are a lot of students who feel ignored. It seems to them that nobody cares, unless they manage to have an eye-catching crisis. For instance, one teenage girl said she did not really want to die, but her suicide attempt was the only way she could get her parents and friends to listen to her cries for help. She was overwhelmed with anxiety and, at times, thought she was losing her mind.

There are many students who believe that nobody cares about them and that school is not a friendly place to be. Teachers are responsible for too many students and classes are often too large. There are not enough counselors or tutors available. Frequently, schools are seen as unfriendly and impersonal.

One way that students can receive timely assistance and feel more a part of their schools is to mobilize student resources—peer facilitators.

Who are Peer Facilitators?

Peer facilitators are students who have received special training enabling them to assist others. Peer facilitators learn concepts and skills in order to help others to think about their feelings and ideas, to explore alternatives, and to make responsible decisions. Other terms have been used to identify peer facilitators, including peer counselors, peer helpers, big brothers and sisters, and peer tutors. Many peer helper groups have adopted a special name for themselves, perhaps related to their school mascots or purpose. In one school, for example, the group was called "Bishop Buddies" and in another it was "Teen Aiders."

One middle school group called themselves the "Fernside Friends," while others have used acronyms to identify themselves, such as:

- ROCS (at Round Rock High School for Realizing Others Care)
- PAL Students (Peer Assistance and Leadership)
- SODA Peer Counselors (Student Organization for Developing Attitudes)
- TIP (Teen Involvement Program)

Although names, projects, responsibilities, and procedures might change from one group to another, the central idea is the same: to help others.

Peer facilitators can be trained at all grade levels, although younger students usually require more supervision, have more limited roles, and take part in more structured activities. Peer facilitator programs in middle and high schools offer more extended training opportunities and, consequently, more involved projects than peer programs in elementary schools. Across age and across grade level helping projects or assignments are common. However, the learned skills can be applied in everyday life outside a designed project or helping activity.

When young people need help, they often turn to their parents or family members for assistance, especially when positive family bonds have been forged in the early years. Mutual respect and admiration in a family can provide a supportive base where assistance can be obtained. Even in the closest knit families, there may not always be enough time (or objectivity) to think through every situation together. Family members may be too caught in their own problems or be experiencing too much stress to be of much help. Some young people may not want to share information with family members for fear of disappointing them or being punished. In cases where families are fragmented by poor personal relationships, separation, divorce, or stressful events, help from the family may be difficult, if not impossible, to obtain.

There are many kinds of helping professions or occupations especially created for personal guidance, such as psychiatry, psychology, and social work. Specialists in these fields try to prevent problems which confront human beings, as well as care for those who are having great difficulties in getting along in the world. They work with students who are having "developmental problems" and they work with "dysfunctional" students who suffer severe stress and who are unable to cope with normal problems.

Families and professional helpers do not have a monopoly on the job of helping others. Sometimes we receive help from a kind stranger, someone who recognizes that we are having problems and who offers a helping hand. A young girl in a store saw that a man was struggling to open a door because his arms were full with packages. She reached over and held open the door for him. He smiled gratefully and acknowledged the help with a simple "Thank you." The help was timely.

A young man was in a library trying to complete a term paper and looking for a special reference book. He needed information from it. Another student noticed how frustrated he was in searching the library files and showed him how to find the book through the new computer system. "Thanks for your help, you saved me a lot of time," he said.

These little moments of helping may not seem important, but they were acts of concern and caring. The helping persons reached out to be of assistance. Their caring acts took no special training, as they shared only their skills and knowledge which they had at the time. Taking time to help someone who can use help is a kind and thoughtful thing to do. You may think of similar occasions where you offered help or received it.

There are times or situations, however, when more skill is useful or even required. This is especially true when we want to help others in their personal and academic development. At those times, interpersonal skills are needed and valuable.

Personal development happens when we have opportunities to think about ourselves. We all can benefit from taking stock of ourselves. We need to take responsibility for whatever we think and do. Because our minds are bombarded with messages from many places and because each of us wants to be our own unique self, it can be useful when someone else helps us think about our choices, our responsibilities, our goals, and our actions.

You can learn to be such a helper. You can learn to facilitate others in the process of thinking about themselves and their worlds. You can facilitate positive growth and development in others and, at the same time, receive some benefits yourself from the helping experiences. As a peer facilitator, you can help people prevent or work through troublesome situations and events in their lives.

The term "peer facilitator" will be used throughout this book. It describes precisely what is expected of you. You are not expected to be a counselor or a therapist, or to assume responsibilities that are typically reserved for trained professionals. The role you will play may be more limited, but no less important or valuable.

In 1978 the American School Counselor Association, the professional organization of school counselors, took the position that peer facilitators could, by assisting counselors in their work, be of service in a school guidance program. It was suggested that almost all students can learn to be facilitators. With special preparation and under supervision, those participating in an organized program could be of great help to peers and create better learning climates in the schools.

The term "peer" is another word that deserves attention. When peer facilitator groups were first started, "peer" indicated that the helpers were from the same age group or school. Yet, in some projects, young peer facilitators have provided assistance to adults, since the learned skills and procedures are appropriate for all people, regardless of age. For instance, one group of high school peer facilitators volunteered to work with lonely senior citizens.

"Peer" has also been used to help differentiate trained skilled helpers from certified or licensed professional helpers. The term "paraprofessional" has been used on occasion, but peer helper or peer facilitator continues to be the most popular term. You will quickly learn, as you go through this book and participate in the learning activities, that your skills can be applied to all human beings. In reality that may be the true meaning of peer.

The Power of Peer Relationships

You may not remember when you were a small child and formed your first friendships. Perhaps it was in the neighborhood, a park, or wherever you came into contact with other children. It is at about the age of three or four that children begin to interact with each other in purposeful ways.

There is no doubt that our parents have a big influence on our lives and how we come to see ourselves. Still, as we grow older, our contemporaries contribute as much or more to our personal and academic development. No matter how much our parents may want to control our experiences, our interactions with our peers eventually become a dominant force in forming our sense of self-worth and well-being. Some of our most enduring values and behaviors in life are formed through our experiences with others in our own age group.

Some parents and adults worry that young people can be led astray by their peers, especially those peers who enjoy defying authorities. Parents are concerned that their children might be negatively influenced by other young people who are involved with drugs, sexual promiscuity, law-breaking activities, or who have poor attitudes about school. However, the evidence suggests that those who grow up in sensitive, caring families with solid bonds, can resist the temptations of being manipulated into antisocial or self-destructive behaviors. Those children who are less fortunate are more susceptible to peer pressure and might be influenced to make poor choices. Working with peer facilitators can help.

Peer relationships are powerful. The desires to be accepted, to be recognized, to be seen as unique and valued, are part of being human. Some young people are consumed with thoughts and actions which they hope will lead to peer acceptance. The desire to be accepted can, in some cases, even be self-destructive or harmful to others.

When peer relationships are positive and the needs and interests of individuals are met within those relationships, then they are even more powerful. Positive relationships cannot be taken for granted. They do not just happen. To the contrary, they are a result of the ways in which people interact with one another. Without knowledge and understanding, good friendships may seem like hit or miss experiences. Sometimes friendly and caring relationships just seem to happen, almost as if by chance. This can be confusing. But, on closer examination, it becomes clear that there are certain elements in positive relationships which make the difference. These elements, and the skills that bring them about, are the focus of study in peer facilitator programs.

Ideally, all students should learn how to be peer facilitators. They would then be better listeners and experience better conversations among themselves and others. They would know how to assist each other, to support each other, and to foster positive relationships at school, at home, and in their communities. They would take more responsibility for their own individual lives and for their own personal development. The rights of all would be enhanced.

Four Basic Helping Roles

Peer facilitators might do many things. They can be of service to many different people. Depending upon their training and experience, they can participate in various kinds of helping projects. There are four different helping roles around which such helping activities can be based: *special assistant, tutor, special friend,* and *small group leader.*

Special assistant

Student assistants work with teachers and counselors in classrooms and in the guidance office or main office. The assistants greet visitors to the school, answer telephones, take messages to teachers and students, construct bulletin boards, help collect or distribute materials or information, and work on routine office or classroom tasks.

Although there is some interaction between peer facilitators and teachers or students, this role is generally confined to providing indirect assistance to peers. The role is limited but often a popular one in schools. It may be the oldest and most traditional helping role that students have assumed in the past.

When peer facilitator training is available, this role can take on new meaning. Even though limited, personal interactions and communication can be improved. School patrols or student hall monitors, for instance, might be more sensitive in giving directions and be more responsive when students have questions or problems. Office workers can learn to greet the public more cordially and to answer telephones more effectively.

Many students are already working in such roles around the school and some of the tasks given student assistants may be performed with little training. But, if they are asked to talk and work closely with people, then peer facilitator training would prove invaluable.

Tutor

Peer tutors work with other students to improve their work in an academic subject. Many research studies have shown that peer tutoring can improve the academic performance of both the students being tutored and the tutors.

While some students are eager to receive assistance, some resist tutoring by another student. One young man said, "If I'm too stupid to learn it from a teacher, what makes you think I can learn from another kid?" This person needed help, but was sensitive to what others might think and say. He was skeptical and not open to learning. It would take a caring and skilled tutor to break through some of his defensiveness and help him get back on track.

Some teachers simply tell a more accomplished student to give some help to a student who is falling behind in class studies. This might work even though not much thought was put into organizing the process. It usually takes more than telling students to work together. To increase success, there needs to be more than a simple match-making of one successful and one less successful student. Being familiar with some basic tutoring techniques and a knowledge of helping skills can make a positive difference. It can speed up the process and make it more effective.

Because some students have persistent problems in their studies, they need more help than a teacher has time to give. On the other hand, these students tend to be resistant, having found studying an unpleasant experience. They might feel embarrassed, guilty, or discouraged and ward off any helping attempts. They may decline assistance at first, thinking that there is little that can be done or worrying that others will think less of them because they need extra help.

While your knowledge and natural instincts for wanting to help someone might be enough, peer facilitator training can show you how to talk with people so that they will give their best efforts. You can learn how to motivate, to encourage, and to help others work through frustration and feelings of defeat.

Peer facilitators working as peer tutors provide a new kind of helping relationship, one that begins by acknowledging what the person is experiencing and how feelings and ideas about self enter into studying.

Special friend

As a special friend, a peer facilitator tries to develop a close helping relationship with another student. This friendship can make the difference for some students who feel they are not involved, left-out, or alienated from school.

For the past several years, surveys of students have shown that the most common problem reported is loneliness. It is singled out above all others. It is the by-product of larger schools, indifferent adults, and fast-paced living. Even those students who are considered popular by their peers find themselves rushing around to be with others in order to avoid being alone and feeling lonely.

Aloneness and loneliness are two separate things. You can be alone and enjoy the solitude, the peace, and the personal time to think, to play music, to read, and to study. Everyone can benefit from alone time, when personal creativeness is given a chance to emerge. On the other hand, loneliness can take place even in a crowd of people.

Loneliness is a result of feeling that nobody cares or is interested in you. It is associated with a feeling of rejection, of being unaccepted, of being devalued. There is an absence of human contact and communication. Moments of loneliness or feeling apart from others is not uncommon and probably everyone has such experiences. It is the intensity of loneliness and its potential for depression which creates the need to have friends. A special friend can make a positive difference, especially when it is beneficial to talk with another person regarding thoughts, feelings, and events.

Being a peer facilitator does not imply that you must become a close, personal buddy with your special friend. This may or may not result from the friendship. Rather, special friends also have a place and time when that friendship can be respected and when they can be together as two interested and caring people. All friendships have boundaries, but each are marked by an attitude of genuine caring, reliable closeness, and mutual respect.

In one high school, some peer facilitators became special friends to young people who were hospitalized, taking time to visit and talk with them. Others have become special friends to new students, to elderly people in retirement homes, and to students who have been identified by teachers as needing someone who will listen to them.

It is in the role of special friends that you might learn about a difficult situation facing the person with whom you are working. The person may confide in you that things are going badly and there is even an element of danger involved. As a peer facilitator your job is not to shoulder all of the burden for fixing problems or making things better.

You will learn through training that there are times when you will be a good listener and treat matters privately. There will be other times when you will confront individuals, perhaps encouraging them to seek out help from an adult or professional. There will be times when you will refer a person to a school counselor, your trainer, or someone who has more authority and more available resources to help. Learning *how* and *when* to refer is part of becoming a peer facilitator.

Small group leader

As small group leaders, peer facilitators can make learning experiences for others more personal and exciting. It can be boring and frustrating to be in a large group and have few opportunities to be heard. Most students want to talk with others about their ideas and share their opinions. We also know that most young people attend classes of 20 or more students. Some are in classes of 30 and 40 or more. There is not enough time for everyone to talk and to be heard unless larger groups are organized into smaller ones.

In order to have smaller groups work efficiently, there must be a designated group leader. When that leader is a trained peer facilitator, group members are more likely to stay on task, to take turns sharing, and to accomplish group goals.

For example, a classroom of 30 students can be divided into six groups of five students each. Six peer facilitators, each assigned to one of the groups, can follow the lead of the teacher or large group leader. At a certain time, the smaller groups can be assembled and each person might be encouraged to say at least one thing about a given topic. Thus, all 30 students participate in a few minutes, rather than a few who dominate a classroom discussion as others sit and listen.

Leading groups as a peer facilitator is also good leadership training. Many of the principles applied in this role can be used in other group situations, either as a leader or as a group member who is trying to help facilitate a group. To be a good leader—a good facilitator—you must know something about how people learn and change.

The Nature of Learning and Changing

How people learn and how they change is a complex subject. Many books have attempted to explain the nature of human behavior and how human beings go about the process of thinking, sensing, and doing. There are many interesting theories and research continues, as each year we learn more about the nature of people and the world in which we live.

Although there is always room for disagreement and other ideas can be added, there appears to be some basic principles about people that lay the foundation for peer helpers and their work. There are central motivators for how we learn and change. Among these are:

- We all have basic needs.
- Everything we do is directed to goals.
- Our self-concepts influence our behaviors.
- Our self-concepts are learned and can change.
- We are always learning and changing.
- Increased self-awareness leads to responsible decision making.
- We learn from each other.

Robert D. Myrick and Betsy E. Folk

We all have basic needs.

We are born with the need to survive. Everything we do is intended to enhance our survival. Even though some behavior is completely unacceptable or not understood, nevertheless it is usually tied to our drive to survive, both physically and psychologically. Our goal, of course, is to learn positive behaviors which meet our needs and which also respect the rights of others to meet their own needs and interests.

The most obvious needs that we all share are those of food, water, elimination, sleep, and shelter. We must meet these needs in our daily lives in order to live. We cannot take them for granted. When people struggle to meet these basic needs, it is hard for them to think about other things. They lose interest in studying, thinking, and discovering more about themselves and others. They are too preoccupied in maintaining their own existence.

After the basic physiological and safety needs are met, individuals are free to pursue other interests and concerns. This does not mean, of course, that one must have the best food or house available or wear designer clothes. There are far too many homeless people in the United States who live in poverty and who do not have adequate diets or clothes. Yet, the vast majority find ways to meet the two basic needs and to move on to higher psychological needs.

Abraham Maslow, a famous psychologist, said that a need-deficient person tends to see others in terms of how they can be used. He believed that "self-actualized persons," whose fundamental needs are met, can respect others and see them as they are—unique human beings with their own problems who can be helped in many ways by various means. Becoming self-actualized, which is a continuing and ongoing process of discovering and appreciating one's self, is a higher order need that everyone has the potential to experience.

Four other personal needs that are noteworthy in the work of peer facilitators are: 1) the need to be loved and accepted; 2) the need for security; 3) the need to belong, and 4) the need to be independent, to take responsibility, and to make choices.

The need to be loved and accepted. We all want to be accepted. While we are similar to others in many ways, we want to see ourselves as unique and we want this uniqueness to be appreciated by others. It is both frustrating and disappointing if we are accepted by others only when we please them.

The need for security. There is a need for us to feel safe and free from threat. We learn best, for example, when we are in situations where others are supportive and encouraging. We tend to be closed to learning when people ridicule us, judge us for our mistakes, or make us feel insecure. There are some students, for example, who are afraid to say what they think for fear that they will be teased or laughed at by their peers. Feeling insecure, these students hesitate to participate in school activities and to take part in class discussions.

The need to belong. All of us want to feel a part of a group, whether it is a family, a school, or a friendship group. Belonging to a group can make us feel accepted and supported. This, in turn, can help reduce anxiety. For instance, there are some students who, upon arriving at school, immediately go to a favorite meeting place where they meet with their friends. Even if it is only for a few minutes, there is a feeling of belonging to a group, a sense of identity. "Hey, what's happening?" is greeted with answers that communicate recognition, acceptance, and shared interest. There are many kinds of groups, some more formal than others. All of them help us to meet the need to belong or to be a part of something.

The need to be independent, to take responsibility, and to make choices. We like to feel that we are in control of our lives and that we have choices. We enjoy the thought of knowing that we are capable of taking care of ourselves and not being dependent on others. Unfortunately, some people who want to be in charge of themselves are unwilling to accept the responsibility that goes with it. They try to shift the blame to others when things do not go right. They look for excuses or believe that they have been treated unfairly. They tend to deceive themselves, taking defensive stands, and try to manipulate others in order to gain a feeling of being in control.

A responsible individual is not afraid to look at alternatives, to consider the consequences, and to make choices that are enhancing to self and to others. We learn how to meet our needs primarily through our parents, our teachers, and other significant people in our lives. We also observe what others say and do, taking note of the consequences and what we can learn from them. We tend to avoid people who are self-destructive or who try to satisfy their needs at our expense. We should look for people who are good models and who are secure enough within themselves that they can help us learn how we can meet our own needs and enjoy life.

There are times, however, when we become confused or disoriented. We are unsure of the best way to meet our needs and we can be fooled into trying shortcuts that lead to dead ends. We are not always perfect and we do make mistakes. Life is too complex to have simple answers that work for everyone, even though there are some guiding principles which can appeal to almost everyone.

Everything we do is directed to goals.

Most of our life we spend time trying to get the most pleasure and the least discomfort. Think about this in terms of your own life. What do you tend to do most often? What do you tend to avoid? What do you hope to achieve? What are your goals? Most of us look to do those things that bring us some type of pleasure or reward. We enjoy pleasant feelings and ideas. We avoid pain, whether it is physical or psychological, and we take precautions so that we will not get hurt. This is true for our psychological self as well as our physical self.

Our day to day living is almost meaningless unless we are striving to achieve some kind of goal. Goals vary from one person to another, but they are always tied to enhancing our way of life.

Our self-concepts influence our behaviors.

An important concept to remember is that we will change our ways to help us survive physically and that we will also change to increase opportunities for our "psychological self" to survive. Thoughts about our own self are generally organized in some way and are consistent. They persist over time and they are often referred to as our "self-concepts."

You have a self-picture of yourself. You know yourself better than anyone else. The picture you have might be described as the "I" or "Me" part of you. It is your self-image or self-concept. It is this part of you that determines your behaviors, what you say, what you tend to think, and what you do. It is the self-concept that interacts with the world. You feel... think... and act based upon your perceptions of life as seen through your self-concept.

Your self-concept is composed of many forms: I *am*—your general nature; I *can*—your abilities; I *should* or *should not*—your beliefs and values; I *want*—your aspirations and desires; and I *will*—your determination to do something. You behave in certain ways because that is the way you see yourself.

You form consistent patterns and habits because they are compatible with how you see yourself. You hang on to certain attitudes and thoughts because to think otherwise would be inconsistent with how you see yourself and this would cause some unpleasant feelings. You feel threatened and can become defensive when others try to tell you who you are, what you are like, and what you are thinking and feeling. "They don't really know me," might be your response. Interestingly, most people never really come to know themselves very well, let alone be known to others. It is a natural tendency to resist change, unless it is in line with how we see ourselves—for better or for worse.

Our self-concepts are learned and can change.

Our self-concepts are formed early in life, especially as we experience the world and receive information from others. We first learn about our self from what others say to us and about us. We take that kind of information, along with our own personal experiences, and try to form some meaning. We look for little clues, anchoring thoughts, which will tell us who we are and how to think, feel, and behave. Of course, the more consistent we are in our thoughts and behaviors, the more cemented our self-picture becomes. This is especially true if our thoughts and behaviors have been rewarded or positively recognized by someone.

Nothing influences the development of our self-concept more than the consequences of our behavior. These consequences shape us and influence the feelings and thoughts that we have, the choices that we make, and the way we interact with others. If the consequences are satisfying, then it is likely that they will be repeated to some degree. If they prove unproductive or dissatisfying in meeting our needs, it is likely that such behaviors will be disregarded or pursued only with reluctance. It is the experiences and consequences of what we do in our daily lives that influence our overall personal style.

A person with a negative self-concept tends to think that tasks are impossible. There is a feeling of "I can't do this." There may also be feelings of rejection or suspicion. Such negative thinking has the person acting in socially ineffective ways, which tends to bring about behaviors from others which are negative. Negative thoughts and behaviors lead to negative consequences, which in turn develop a negative picture of self and life. It is a vicious cycle.

On the other hand, if a person has a positive self-concept, then there is a feeling that things will turn out all right and that success is just around the corner. It is easier to approach tasks or to be with other people. There is a self-assurance and self-confidence that tends to generate productive behaviors, which are subsequently rewarded or recognized. This encourages the person to behave similarly in the future, out of positive thoughts and feelings, which increases the person's chance for success. Another cycle is put into place, but it is much different and more effective than the first.

Robert D. Myrick and Betsy E. Folk

We are always learning and changing.

A lot of people believe that all learning takes place at home, in school, or in a place of religious worship. In reality, learning is taking place everywhere all the time. It is not limited to a certain place or when you are with a teacher. You watch, you listen, and you talk with others about all kinds of things. You take in information from your surroundings and you interact with your environment. You are always learning.

Learning, naturally, is more than memorizing facts or collecting pieces of information. It is more than what you remember from your class textbooks or from what your teachers have told you. It is the very act of living and surviving.

We are not always motivated to learn and, consequently, our readiness for learning may be low. That is, what we notice and recall may be limited by our personal involvement in the learning process. If we are unaware of ourselves and others, or of our environment, then learning takes place at a very low level, perhaps minimally at an unconscious state. Because we are not involved, what we learn may have little meaning and may not appear to be of much value.

A teenage girl thought she was learning nothing by attending a math class. She was bored and hated the class. She knew in her own mind that everyone thought she was dumb. She doodled most of the time and tried to sleep when she could.

She dreaded going to class and would skip it as much as she could. Although she did not learn much math, since she did not experience it or work with the ideas, she was learning about how to survive in such a situation. Her avoidance behaviors and negative attitudes were reinforced since they were successful. She did not let the daily lessons or class meetings get through her defenses. "Who needs it?" "I'm not going to use this stuff." "Besides, the teacher thinks I'm stupid and he's about the worst teacher I've ever had." "I can't see how the other kids can stand him.... He thinks he's strict, so tough, but I'm not afraid of him."

Eventually, she was removed from the class and no longer threatened by the experience. Did she learn anything? She did. However, her own level of personal awareness may not have helped her identify what she learned most from the class, which may have been how to make excuses, to avoid work, and to avoid taking responsibility.

"I can't change; there isn't any use; I've tried." Some people feel defeated and believe that things will always be the same. This can be a trap, for change is inevitable. You cannot remain the same person. Time moves on and you are always in the process of changing. You may choose to remain basically the same person with the same kind of style or habits, or you can try to influence the changes that come in life.

The most obvious evidence of change is found in our communities, as we watch new buildings going up and old ones falling down. Repairs are made to buildings and also to people. People become older and, sometimes, they are more receptive to learning. Some become more tolerant of themselves and others, while some grow even more bigoted and self-centered. Nevertheless, change is always taking place. We are not always aware of it.

There are some very consistent patterns about our personalities that are formed early in life which tend to endure. Patterns of living, little habits, and tendencies toward certain thoughts or feelings are a result of stable self-concepts which have been developed. Still, we can and do change. We can be influenced by others. In some instances, change is slow, even when we want to speed up the process and become impatient.

Too many times, our self-concepts resist change, especially when they have become comfortable—for better or for worse. Yet, the change process, while inevitable, is not always easy to manage. Management becomes easier when we know more about ourselves and others. There are cases where people have realized that they want to change—they want to become somebody else. They want to learn a new style of life and push the old one into the past, to be forgotten or ignored. These people may have encountered a special person, or been part of an inspiring event, or perhaps reached a stage in life where they could become more responsible and more open to change.

Increased self-awareness leads to responsible decision making.

Some people go through life, quite happy at times, without much awareness of who they are, what they want out of life, where they want to go, or what they want to happen. They are content to go with the flow of things, to react rather than initiate, or to find comfort in some reliable and consistent habits and patterns. Their awareness of self and others is limited, but they are content.

Other people take more charge of their lives and enjoy taking an active part in making decisions and finding ways to take action. They want to be more aware of the events that are taking place around them, believing that increased awareness gives them more information upon which to make decisions. They want to know more about themselves and others so that they know what factors are influencing their choices, their decisions, and their actions. They want the satisfaction of knowing that they have looked at all the possibilities.

If we lack a sense of self-awareness, we may find ourselves acting or reacting out of habit or convenience. We may avoid taking a stand for fear that we would contradict ourselves. We would lack self-confidence because we could not predict our chances of success and would certainly feel less in control of our lives. The world would seem like a magic wonderland, if not a frightening jungle. It would be difficult to separate fantasy from reality. Instead of taking responsibility, there would be a tendency to dismiss the world as a place of whim, luck, or of uncontrollable events. It might be easier to follow the crowd.

Those who value self-awareness take time to reflect on their circumstances, to analyze contributing factors, to set goals and priorities, and then to act in responsible ways. They are contributors. They are, among others, our best teachers, leaders, family members, and friends.

We learn from each other.

Unless you are dedicated to being a hermit and avoiding all contact with the outside world, including books, you cannot help but learn from others. Even as you read this book, you are learning something, regardless of whether you agree or disagree with what is being said to you through the printed words. Even to disagree is to provide an opportunity to test an idea—an hypothesis. To agree is perhaps nothing more than confirming what you have already learned, heard, or believed. The real learning is a personal one—one that is taking place as you interact with the authors of this text.

Most of what we learn comes through our interactions with others. It can be from a book in the solitude of an evening while sitting on the bank of a lake, or it can be in a classroom, where a discussion is taking place about current events. It can happen when on a school bus, as you watch two people fight over a particular seat. It can also happen at the dinner table, while watching television, or simply sharing ideas with a friend. Learning is involvement and it usually means interacting with others.

Learning need not be a one-way street. You cannot help someone else learn without learning more about yourself. The level of awareness of that learning, of course, may differ from one person to another, as well as from one situation to another. Some teachers, for example, believe that they cannot learn anything new because they have taught the same lesson over and over. These are not your best teachers. They are unaware of what is happening in the class—the way in which students are learning. The most effective teachers never tire of a lesson because they know that there is always something else to be learned or experienced. They learn from the students and the students learn from them.

As a peer facilitator, you will learn from those with whom you have an opportunity to help. You may assume that because you do not have a similar problem or have never been in similar circumstances that there is nothing to be learned. You are going to be in for a surprise. What one person learns in a given situation may be different from someone else.

Facilitating others is a learning process—it is a two-way street. You will not only be giving something of yourself, but you will be receiving something of value in return. You will have the satisfaction of touching another life in a positive way. Perhaps this is the heart of peer helping and the most powerful reward.

Activity 1.1
Challenging Problems

Purpose: To increase awareness of the problems which face youth.
Materials: Pencil/pen

Procedures:

1. On your own, examine the ten problem areas listed below. Decide which ones you believe are of major concern to students in your school. Put a "1" in the blank next to the most significant one.

2. Then, continue using numbers to rank the others.

3. There will be ten positions in the room, perhaps from left to right, numbered from 1 to 10. This will be the scale on which you can stand to show how you ranked the different problems.

4. After everyone in the room has ranked the problems individually, the classroom leader will call out a problem area (e.g. getting good grades in school). Students move silently and quickly to the numbers located in the room which correspond to the rank that they gave the problem.

5. In a class discussion, students in each numbered area share the reasons they ranked the problem area as they did.

6. After the first problem area has been "group ranked," the second problem area is announced and, again, students move to the numbered areas to show their rankings.

7. Continue the same procedures with each of the problem areas.

Ten challenging problems: ____Feeling lonely or isolated

   ____Getting good grades in school   ____Use of alcohol

   ____Getting along with parents   ____Choosing a career

   ____Making and keeping friends   ____Use of illegal drugs

   ____Boy/girl relationships   ____Cliques and gangs

                                           ____Racial and ethnic issues

Key Questions:

What are some of the reasons given for the rankings? On which issues do the class most agree? Disagree? Is there another problem area which you would add? How are these problems different from the ones that adults have? What about younger students?

                                               Robert D. Myrick and Betsy E. Folk

Activity 1.2
Who are the Helpers?

Purpose:

To identify the different helpers to whom students often turn when they have problems.

Materials:

None

Procedures:

1. Look at this list of ten helpers:

    ____Teacher

    ____Counselor

    ____Doctor

    ____Friend

    ____Parent

    ____Minister or clergy

    ____Neighbor

    ____Relative

    ____Principal

    ____Police Officer

2. Which three of the helpers listed above, in rank order, would you turn to *first* if you had a problem? More specifically, which three—in order—would you go to if the problem were about:

    A. Conflict with a certain teacher

          1. _____ 2. _____ 3. _____

    B. Feeling lonely and depressed

          1. _____ 2. _____ 3. _____

    C. Alcohol and drugs

          1. _____ 2. _____ 3. _____

    D. Sex

        1. _____ 2. _____ 3. _____

    E. Family conflict

        1. _____ 2. _____ 3. _____

    F. Career

        1. _____ 2. _____ 3. _____

3. Pair up with another student in class and discuss your rankings.

Key Questions:

What influenced you to select a particular helper? What would you expect that person to do? Is there a pattern in your choices? Who is left out most often? What other issues face young people and who are the helpers?

Robert D. Myrick and Betsy E. Folk

Chapter 2

Helping and Enhancing Relationships

The word "relationship" means a lot of different things and can be used in a variety of ways. A math teacher may ask, "What relationship does the circle have with the sphere?" A social studies teacher might inquire, "Can you see the relationship between these two political issues?" These teachers are asking how these shapes or issues are connected or about the conditions that they have in common.

In communication, the term relationship refers to the ways in which people interact with others. Almost everyone is interested in how interpersonal relationships work. What makes people do things? Why are some people more likable than others? How can close friendships be formed? How do people influence one another?

Human Nature and Relationships

It is human nature to seek out and develop relationships with others. There are some personal needs that can only be satisfied through interactions with other human beings. Much of the joy, success, and meaning in life that we experience is related to how well we have formed positive relationships with others.

Interpersonal relationships begin as soon as we are born, even though as babies we cannot use words to express ourselves. When we are born into families, we learn from family members how to eat, to talk, to play, and to work. We learn how to get along with others.

Even if we were not with our biological parents, there was someone who took care of us, nurtured us, and taught us something about people. Some parents or guardians are more positive than others, but relationships in our early years taught us how to relate with people, to communicate, and to meet our needs.

Our personal relationships change as we grow older. Even relationships between our parents or guardians change. With each passing day, there is new information, different events, more experience, practiced skills, and new emerging needs. In time, we form new relationships outside the family, perhaps with other relatives, neighbors, or people in the community. In school we form personal relationships with significant adults and peers and our personal growth continues.

Even though we are dependent upon others and need to relate with them, we are not born knowing instinctively how to interact effectively. The drive to be with and to know people—to be recognized and to communicate—is present in all of us. But, the basic interpersonal skills, such as being sensitive to others and relating effectively to them, are *learned.*

We first learned basic communication skills because they were modeled for us by our parents, teachers, and peers. We observed and filed away ideas and information which we thought would help us meet our needs and to survive. In school there are opportunities to observe, to read, and to talk about how people relate with one another. Sometimes there is a chance to study and practice skills, such as in a peer facilitator training program or life management skills class. Sometimes, unfortunately, it is a case of trial and error. That is, we learn by our mistakes. Can you think of times when you did not communicate very well with someone else? Maybe you can recall a time when your relationship with others caused problems for you and for them.

Kinds of Relationships

Since relationships are so essential for our personal well-being and the well-being of our society, it might be helpful to think of how the term "relationship" is used in everyday life. For instance, politicians might say that they are worried about their relationships with the voters. A woman may enter a marriage relationship with a man who had two children by a previous marriage and wondered what kind of relationship would develop between her and the step-children. Two teenagers, working in a fast food store, might quit their jobs because the working relationships were so unpleasant.

For the most part, "relationship" refers to how people are either legally related or how they interact with others. There are different kinds of relationships.

Formal or informal relationships

Some relationships are considered formal because they may have come about through legal measures. Some resulting relationships defined by law are:

- Wife—husband
- Father—mother—children
- Brother—sister
- Daughter or brother in-law
- Uncle or aunt
- Grandfather and grandmother
- Step-father or mother
- Step-sister or brother
- Cousins
- Child—guardian

This is a matter of identifying blood relationships, formalized by governmental statutes. By law we are sometimes impelled to be considered part of a family, connected through legal procedures. In many cases, there is no choice. The relationship simply comes about because of circumstances.

Other relationships are considered formal because of the recognized status and roles of the people in a particular situation. Teacher—student, doctor—patient, attorney—client, or salesperson—customer might be examples of formal relationships where an expected interaction usually takes place between the parties. It is generally formal, structured, and within assigned or agreed upon roles. All seem to know their parts, functions, and limits. But even in cases where roles within the formal relationships appear to be carefully spelled out, there can be conflicts and problems.

Informal relationships result from spontaneous events or circumstances. They are often more social and relaxed. There are no defined roles or guidelines which direct people to act in certain ways. There are no expectations. People are usually together by choice. Of course, within these kinds of relationships the degree of closeness and involvement may vary.

A group of people may end up being in close proximity and be interested in the same goal, such as watching a football game or movie. The relationships can be so informal and distant that the people are only faintly aware of others being present.

There is little or no attempt to interact, even though they might join in similar activities (e.g. cheering for a favorite team).

Within this group, however, there are likely to be smaller groups which feel a closer alliance. Perhaps they know each other from other situations and through familiarity have formed a circle of acquaintances or close friends. Participation and investment in a group usually depends on whether it is personal or impersonal.

Personal or impersonal relationships

Some people have common experiences and interact in such a way that they feel connected. There is a mutual affinity for talking and sharing ideas and a desire to be close. There is a personal feeling of belonging. This may occur between two people or in a group.

In an impersonal group, members are in close proximity but do not feel connected. They may be in the same group but they have the feeling that they do not know anyone there. Regardless of the circumstances which have brought them together (e.g. school, club), there is no special bond. Even though they are aware that others are near, there is a separateness. There is a feeling of being disassociated, perhaps even isolated. In these impersonal groups, people tend to guard themselves and avoid being involved.

Being part of a group of people is an inevitable part of life. Unless you live in a remote part of the country where there are few people, being a member of different kinds of groups is inevitable. You cannot avoid it. You can, however, avoid getting involved and feel detached. The extent to which a group is designed to be personal or impersonal, and your own involvement, can be affected by the way in which you and other members interact with one another.

Enhancing or destructive relationships

For fear of being hurt or experiencing some kind of discomfort, some people try to avoid getting involved with people. They feel safer in their own shell, content to be by themselves. If by chance they are forced into being a part of a group (e.g. community, neighborhood, church, school), they may resist attempts to know others or to be an active member. They may even become a destructive force or barrier to those who want to form closer relationships and make the group more personal.

If enough members of a group resist associating with one another, or direct all their efforts to keeping their distance, remaining separate and staying uninvolved, it is possible that a few members of a group may dominate and, for better or for worse, be responsible for the direction in which the group takes. Leadership emerges in every group, sometimes lodged in the hands of a few and at other times in the group as a whole. Have you ever been in a group where you felt you were a passive member, going along with the flow of events as directed by others?

A few groups, void of positive leadership, can become destructive. For example, the infamous Nazi party in Germany years ago led many willing people astray. With special hopes and promises, countless numbers of individuals were deceived into thinking that the world would be better if all the party's policies were implemented. However, only a few insiders knew that the group was headed by a power base which served the interests of a few and became a nightmare for others.

On a smaller scale, there are family groups that are destructive. Members attack each other, verbally and physically. They coerce weaker family members to do as they are told and give them little or no voice in matters. Likewise, the same might be true of schools or clubs where the general feeling is one of being forced to do things against one's will, one's values, or to comply simply because others are in positions of greater strength and power.

Teenage gangs in cities are formed because they provide an identity for its members, who want to experience the feeling of belonging. They want recognition and to feel special. These groups can act in productive ways when they think positively and take pride in themselves and their communities. On the other hand, they may be a destructive force when they feel alienated.

In a negative alliance, gang members try to gain power by demeaning others. They vandalize, commit crimes, and hurl insults at people. They do whatever they can to feel superior, gaining a false sense of strength and pride, at the expense of others. Because they are closely affiliated with each other, there is a feeling of power, control, identity, and success, even though it may be self-destructive in the long run.

Destructive type groups thrive on threat, fear, divisiveness, a lack of respect for others and themselves, punishment, denial of rights, insensitive leadership, and uncaring attitudes. There is a defensiveness which keeps the group from growing in positive ways or allowing members to be accepted and valued for their uniqueness. Within such groups, interactions force individuals to blindly conform, to become hesitant and suspicious, and to sacrifice their personal potential.

Such destructiveness in groups may exist on a national level, such as in a country or state. It may be a part of a national organization, spreading across many miles. It may be representative of a community in which people live. It might be found in schools, classes, teams, or places of employment. It may even be found in what some see as close-knit families.

When personally destructive forces dominate a group and form its character, the potential for self-development and the improvement of relations between people is thwarted. Positive potential may never be realized, thus affecting the well-being of its individuals and society.

Enhancing type groups are just the opposite. They too can be found everywhere—in nations, communities, schools, classes, and families. They are characterized by a different set of forces which operate within them.

Members of enhancing groups feel safe and secure, knowing that their participation is valued. They sense that each member can contribute and that the participation of all makes the whole group better. Although they may not be related in blood and flesh, there is a kindred feeling of being a part of a closely related group. The rights of an individual are respected and honored as group decisions are based on democratic principles, giving everyone an opportunity to participate, to be involved, to express themselves, and to be heard. Members do not have to agree or even support group decisions, but they recognize that the purpose for the group being together and the way people interact within the group gives them a sense of togetherness and well-being.

When family members, for example, interact with each other in such a way as to create an enhancing atmosphere, every family member experiences acceptance and respect. There is more cooperation, since each member's rights are protected and honored. Even though at times an individual is out voted and must go along with the wishes of others, there is a desire to see that each member is given as much leeway as possible to achieve personal goals, to maximize personal potential. This kind of family knows how to resolve conflicts through interpersonal skills.

You can play an important part in the groups to which you belong. You can help facilitate a group toward its goals and help facilitate the interaction of others. You can be an enhancing member of an enhancing group.

Helpful or nonhelpful relationships

There are times when people want to be helped. They might have reached an impasse in their lives and are unsure of what to do next. They need an opportunity to think things through, searching for some kind of insight that will help them develop a plan. They may simply need a kind and caring friend who will listen to them as they vent their feelings.

People who work with things (such as machinery, appliances, equipment, or factory goods) may think that they have less experience or opportunities to deal with people. One person said, "My job is to provide services, to make repairs, and to fix things. I'm not a people person." Yet, the most valued workers whose jobs deal with *things* rather than *people* know how to interact with others. They know how to make the best of the limited time that they have with customers or others on the job in order to improve services. They want satisfied customers and pleasant working conditions.

When morale on a job is low and when people who work together on a project (e.g. in factory or company) feel alienated from fellow workers, production can be hampered. Absenteeism increases, job complaints are prevalent, and loyalty to the company can be absent. Job relationships are important. Interpersonal skills permeate all of our society, including places where interaction among people is limited.

Robert D. Myrick and Betsy E. Folk

One wealthy businessman who owns a chain of stores makes a point of thanking his workers when they work on holidays. He knows that they are taking time away from their families on days when other families make it a point to be together. He takes time to let them know how much he particularly appreciates their working on those special days. Workers report that he is an owner who cares about them and their well-being. He creates a family feeling among employees, who in turn support each other and do their best to provide services to customers.

There are other jobs where working with people becomes the primary condition of employment and people skills are given high priority (e.g. salespeople, teachers, politicians, clergy, counselors). These skills are used to help people. There is an emphasis on building, rebuilding, and maintaining enhancing relationships.

What kind of relationship does it take before you can talk seriously with someone about matters? How do you know if the person will take you seriously and, rather than argue or fight with you, encourage you to think more about the issues?

In a helpful relationship, there is an exchange of ideas. There is mutual interest and respect. While unpleasant ideas and feelings can be expressed, there is a sense of support. The togetherness that is present is a kind of partnership which is, even for a brief time, thoughtful and productive. One is not pushed or forced into something. In non-helpful relationships, there are feelings of resistance and disinterest, if not begrudging compliance.

One student who had a non-helpful relationship with some friends said, "My buddies tried to talk me into quitting school, but it seemed senseless; so, I stopped talking with them. Eventually, I quit hanging around with them." A student who had a helpful relationship reported, "My best friend is great! She seems to know what I'm going through and, no matter what I do—and I've done some pretty dumb things—I know she will be there to help me when I need her. She's just a neat friend and I don't know what I would I do without her."

Building and Maintaining Relationships

Your social world expanded dramatically after you started attending school. It was probably in kindergarten and the primary grades that you were first introduced to other children and to organized experiences with people outside the family. As you have grown older, the day to day school experiences have made an undeniable impression. Part of those experiences are beyond what the school curriculum had planned for you. You have been a part of a group of learners, interacting with them and your teachers.

One's identity as a person is built from relationships with other people, for better or for worse. As you work, play, and take part in routine activities with others, you also take note of how people respond to you. Quite often you come to view yourself as others see you, based on the feedback that they give you.

As you try to make sense out of the world, you have come to depend on others to validate your perceptions and impressions. While you can touch a flower, smell it, and chart its growth, you cannot always be sure of the realities in a world of people that is made up of values, rules, procedures, ideas, and feelings. These are not fixed or tangible things. What is beautiful or ugly? What is fair or unfair? What is the best way or the worst way? In order to make the most sense out of life, we need to be with other people, to share our perceptions and reactions with them. We need to know what others are thinking, feeling, and doing, and to see how their perceptions match or differ from our own.

Some adults and young people have trouble working with others. They struggle to communicate and they are often misunderstood. They themselves frequently misinterpret the actions of others and become suspicious and incommunicative. In their separateness, they sometimes feel that nobody cares. They become hateful and destructive towards themselves and sometimes towards others. They need help in feeling that they are a part of society and that through relearning and new learning they can be productive citizens. They need some positive interpersonal experiences.

A great deal of living life positively depends on the actions that take place in a society which is made up of many kinds of groups. We are social beings and most of our happiness or misery is based on the liking that people have for us. The extent to which we feel loved and loving, cared for and caring, involved and active, compassionate and concerned, considerate and responsive, will determine the quality of our lives and our nation. To enjoy life, and to provide for our future, and the future of those who will follow us, perhaps nothing is more important than our interpersonal relationships. You can play a role in improving relationships in and out of school.

Robert D. Myrick and Betsy E. Folk

The Helping Relationship

Sometimes people just seem to get along "fabulously." They "hit it off," perhaps from the first time that they met. There is a friendliness, a bond, which develops instantly. "We're just on the same wave length, like we know what each of us is thinking." When asked to explain further, the people often struggle for the exact words to describe their friendship or the closeness that they feel. They simply know that there is a special bond that has developed.

Then, there are other people who make unfavorable impressions. Right from the beginning there is a feeling of distance, perhaps even a desire to avoid any personal relationship. But, given the right circumstances, these same people might come to know each other better and to discover their common interests, needs, and connections. As they take note of each other, the relationship has the potential for growing more positively and they come to develop a valued friendship.

In some instances, relationships between people are so fractured that there appears to be a dislike for even sharing the same general area. There is an adversary relationship, competing for attention, ignoring the other person, disdaining all contributions, and being insensitive to the needs of the other person. There are no close ties and, consequently, they have little positive impact on each other. Their relationship is unproductive and barely tolerable. Such relationships have been reported among some family members, classmates, teachers and students, and young and older people in a community.

We have known for a long time that some relationships are more helpful and encouraging than others. Carl Rogers, a pioneering counseling theorist, believed that if certain human conditions existed between people, then a helping process would automatically be set into motion. This process would help people realize their potential, including taking responsibility for and solving their own problems. He said that certain personal conditions were essential and sufficient to produce positive changes in people.

Not everyone has agreed that the conditions alone are sufficient in and by themselves or that nothing else is needed. However, almost everyone in the business of helping others recognizes that Rogers touched on the same ideas that seem to make an important difference in helping people. If you are seen, for example, as a friendly and caring person, then others are more likely to want to be with you—to talk with you. If they see you as a careful listener, someone who is respectful, understanding, and interested in what they have to say, then they will probably want to explore their feelings and ideas with you—to discuss their goals and possible choices with you.

In our busy day to day living, where everyone seems to be rushing through events, it is not easy to find helping relationships which enable people to think about matters in depth-relationships and which provide the security of knowing that one's ideas and feelings are treated with respect and care. There are not enough helpers who have time to create the helping conditions.

Six Facilitative Conditions

A helping relationship can be developed if certain kinds of facilitative conditions, as we will call them, are present. These conditions are considered facilitative because they encourage people to self-disclose, to be open to ideas and choices, and to consider feedback from others. A long list of ideal conditions might be presented, but that might make you think that an effective helper has to be a saint or an extraordinary individual in order to facilitate the personal growth of others. This is not the case.

There are a few facilitative conditions that seem to characterize the work of effective peer facilitators. Among these are: *1) caring; 2) understanding; 3) acceptance; 4) respect; 5) friendliness;* and *6) trustworthiness*. Let us take a closer look at each of them.

Caring

A caring person takes personal interest in someone else and shows concern about that person's well-being. You have to give something of yourself, perhaps reaching out and showing that you are committed to helping that person. You have to care enough to get involved, which is the heart of being a peer facilitator.

Understanding

This term is used to acknowledge that you know what the other person is experiencing. That is, you may not fully know the events or have a grasp of what is taking place in someone's life, but you do have an idea of what they are feeling. There is an awareness on your part that you sense what the other person is going through, even though you may not know the details of the situation. It goes beyond knowledge of events and focuses on moods and emotions.

"Put yourself in their shoes," is a popular expression when people are being encouraged to be sensitive to others. "You will never understand someone unless you have walked the same miles, been on the same journey." This probably is true, if the goal is to fully know what the person has experienced and to be totally aware of all the details that went into the events that took place. But, being understanding does not mean that you have to assume that person's role or to have been that person. In fact, there may not be much advantage to it.

One peer facilitator was trying to show that he understood what someone was talking about. He kept asking questions, trying to get more information about what took place. His interest about the situation was admirable, but hardly understanding. Understanding is more than being able to repeat words or to describe events as accurately as the one telling the story. Rather, understanding implies that you grasp what the person is experiencing or feeling. You have a sense of the emotions that resulted from the actual events and from the telling of the story.

In order to be understanding, you must not only listen to the words which describe the events of the story, for they are important, but you must be able to go beyond the words and be aware of the feelings that go with those words. When you communicate that you are aware of the person's feelings, you have gone a long way toward establishing the helping relationship.

Acceptance

You may not agree with something that a person has said or done. You may find that you disagree with how the person sees things, or even what the person values. Acceptance of the person, however, suggests that you still believe in the dignity and worth of that person. It is assumed that accepting people as human beings who are doing the best that they can with what they know and feel is an essential step to helping. It is further assumed that people's behaviors can be challenged when they sense that you still value them as human beings and want to know more about them.

This may sound easier than it is. Your own values, interests, and needs will come into play as you listen to someone talk about a situation. As the person continues to relate the story, you may find yourself wanting to pass judgment (that was right or that was wrong) or evaluate (that was good or that was bad).

There is a natural tendency for us to approve and accept those things that are most like us. We can identify with them and see them as being natural or normal. Likewise, we tend to ignore or reject those things that are alien or foreign to us. If something is unfamiliar, we frequently find ourselves becoming alert and defen-sive. Differences are threatening, especially when they challenge the comfort of our own life style.

The more we know about ourselves, the more secure we are and the more self-confident we can be when working with others. When we hear something that is out of the ordinary, or perhaps out of our own experience, we need to work hard at staying open. This can best be done if we accept the other person, which can then lead to understanding. The fundamental part of acceptance is a belief that every individual is unique and they all are doing the best that they can do to meet their needs and to get along in this world.

We must accept the fact that they are human, that they are trying to survive the best way that they can, that whatever they do they have learned from somewhere, and that they are also capable of change. If we can somehow communicate that acceptance, then we are also free to challenge their behaviors, to encourage them to think and to explore, and, if appropriate, urge them to change.

Respect

Most people expect a few common courtesies when they are with other people. They want to have an opportunity to tell their side of the story or share their perceptions, rather than being "talked at." They have the right to their own feelings, to express their own ideas, and to be responsible for their own decisions and to shape their own lives. They want to be treated with respect.

Friendliness

You can communicate friendliness through your own personal style. A smile, a warm greeting, kindly gestures, good eye contact, and a friendly attitude can do a lot to promote a helping relationship. Friendliness helps facilitate a person because it is inviting and opens the door for other facilitative conditions which may take time to communicate.

Trustworthiness

Trusting someone can mean many things. It might, for instance, indicate how well you can predict someone's actions. "I trust him to come through for me when things are tough," said one student about a close friend. "I don't trust anyone, " said one cynical student, "because everyone is out to get you—to use you." This student thought it was impossible to rely on others for help, since they could not be trusted. If you trust some people, it usually means that you believe that those persons will not hurt you, that they will not take whatever information that they have about you and use it against you. Most people want a straight-forward, honest relationship where they feel secure. Being trustworthy inspires confidence and encourages openness.

Summary

These facilitative conditions are not limited to your work as a peer facilitator. They can be a part of all interpersonal relationships, between students and teachers, children and parents, and class-mates. They are so important that we will take time to increase our awareness of them, to study them, and to think of ways in which we can make them happen in our work with others.

Relationships, then, can be of many kinds. The helping relationship can be provided by a professional helper, or someone who is committed to helping someone else and who knows how to be a facilitator. Helping relationships are best characterized by the six facilitative conditions. When these conditions are present, there is a better chance that some positive things are going to happen. Both the one being helped and the helper feel like working together, exploring ideas, and arriving at some possible solutions to problems. If the helping relationship is the center of peer helping and if the facilitative conditions are central to the helping relationship, what must be done to bring them about? What must you do as a facilitator?

Activity 2.1
I've Got a Secret

Purpose:

To become more aware of the facilitative conditions.

Materials:

Paper and pencil

Procedures:

1. Think of a secret, something that you have not told anyone else. It may be something that you have done, or something you have thought about doing. Just in case you are wondering, you are not going to be asked to write the secret down or tell it to anyone. But, take a few seconds and think about your secret.

2. Now, look around the class or group. Think about who is here and what you know about them. What would you need from them before you would be willing to tell your secret to everyone? Now, write one word or phrase that will describe what you need.

3. The slips of paper are collected by the class leader or trainer. The words are listed and summarized on the chalkboard. All thoughts, even if they are silly or seemingly inappropriate, are noted.

4. Discuss the responses which have been listed and why they are important.

Key Questions

Were any of the six facilitative conditions of helping relationships (i.e., caring, understanding, acceptance, respect, friendliness, and trust) mentioned? What makes confidentiality so important to some people? How is it different from being trustworthy and treating matters privately?

Activity 2.2
What's in a Relationship?

Purpose:

To become more aware of different kinds of relationships and the value of helping relationships.

Materials:

None

Procedures:

1. The class is divided into three working groups.

2. One group is assigned the task of demonstrating both formal and informal relationships at a party. The second group has the task of showing both enhancing and destructive relationships between a parent and child. The third group demonstrates both helpful and nonhelpful relationships between a teacher and a student.

3. After each group presentation, a class discussion focuses on the behaviors, language, and attitudes of those demonstrating the two contrasting types of relationships.

Key Questions:

How did you feel in the different roles? Are some roles or behaviors always related to a particular relationship? Is it possible to have more than one kind of a relationship with a parent? A close friend? A teacher? How would you describe a helping relationship?

Awareness of Self and Others

Despite the fact that we live in a world of over five billion people, each of us is unique. We are uniquely different in terms of our physical and psychological combinations. We often share similar beliefs and attitudes with others, yet there are special feelings, thoughts, reactions, and experiences which are especially ours.

When we were infants, we did not know much about ourselves. As we grew older, experiences with parents, teachers, and friends influenced the way in which we came to see ourselves. Through our experiences, we developed a self-picture or a self-concept.

The Nature of Self

The way you see and feel about yourself is referred to as your "self-concept." If you feel loved and successful, then you will think positive thoughts about yourself and view yourself as worthwhile. If you believe that you are undesirable, unloved, and have negative thoughts about yourself, then you may have a poor self-concept. The things you do and say are the result of your self-concept.

It is important to remember that our self-concept is *learned*. From the time we are born, we start collecting and accumulating information about ourselves and the world in which we live. We form impressions about others. We learn what brings pain and pleasure-what makes us happy or dissatisfied. It is molded on a day to day basis with those significant others in our lives.

From the time you were an infant, you began thinking thoughts about yourself. You learned your name and realized that you were separate from those around you. While you needed special care, it was not long before you were saying, "Me, do it." As time passed, the "me" became a person with special interests and needs.

By the time you reached school age, you already had a consistent self-picture. It had been formed through many successes and failures in every day life. It had been colored by comments which people made to you. Slowly but surely, your own attitudes and personal beliefs developed, and these too influenced the way in which you interpreted the events around you.

Because you receive so much information about yourself, it is not always easy to gain a clear picture of self. Sometimes, the information is accurate and worthwhile. At other times, it is vague and uncertain. You might find the information confusing. Still at other times, you may find the information inaccurate. Regardless, all the information tends to have an impact on your self-development and the eventual formation of your self-concept.

Even though your self-concept tends to be consistent, it is always in the process of changing. As you grow older, there are new experiences in life which influence you. In addition, like others, you are a complex human being with many feelings and ideas who can play many roles. Sometimes these roles are fun and challenging and, at other times, they are mysterious or confusing, depending on the situation.

Sometimes it is possible to think of yourself as a master of disguise. One day, you might be wearing a frolicking, happy costume with a cheerful mask. All the world appears to be fun-loving and a happy place to be. On other days, you may be wearing a mask of sadness or worry, and the world may seem gray and dreary.

The formation of your self-concept is influenced daily by your experiences. In order to get along in the world-to feel successful-you may try on different costumes or masks. The masks that you tend to choose most often, for some reason or another, are those that have made you feel secure.

Angela was having trouble understanding her math lesson. She asked several questions in class and left feeling pleased that she now could complete her assignment. Then, she overheard two of her classmates say, "Angela asks the dumbest questions in class. She doesn't seem to understand anything." Can you imagine how Angela felt? One minute she is feeling positive about herself, and the next minute she is being confronted by the negative thoughts of others. Will her classmates comments change how Angela sees herself?

Who are *You?*

We realize that our self is comprised of a vast array of variables. Our identity, or who we think we are, is determined by many things.

First, you are either a male of a female. With that particular distinction of gender, you begin the process of defining your identity. If you are a male, then you are automatically cast into certain gender roles: son, brother, boyfriend, husband, and father. If you are female, the roles would be: daughter, sister, girlfriend, mother, and wife. In addition, there are some gender stereotypes which are held up as models, for better or for worse, which in turn influence your thinking about self. How has being either male or female affected the way you think about yourself?

Our self-picture is molded by our race and cultural heritage. We live in a multi-cultural society which respects racial and cultural differences. Being a Caucasian, African-American, Hispanic, Oriental, or Indian will invariably affect a person's self-concept. There will always be individual uniqueness within each of these groups; nevertheless, racial and cultural history cannot be ignored.

For instance, a young Indian girl in high school, Tasneen, chose to wear her sari, or outer garment, to school each day. The tradition is a part of her culture. It is expected of her and something she has come to accept. Even though it is unusual dress compared to the majority of students, it is part of Tasneen's self-concept and she would be uncomfortable wearing anything else.

Religious beliefs can affect how persons see the world, their role in the world, and perhaps even their role after they die. Jennifer is a high school senior who bases her decisions on what to do on the weekends in relationship to her religious beliefs. She stated, "I am a Christian, and my body is a temple according to the *Bible*. I choose to follow my religious convictions and not smoke or drink. I can still have a good time just being with my friends." How do your religious values or personal beliefs affect how you feel about yourself?

Your psychological self-picture (self-concept) can also be influenced by your physical stature and characteristics. Do you see yourself as too tall, too short, or just right? Do you like the color of your hair and eyes? Do you think you weigh too much or too little? Do you call yourself "thin," "fat," "ugly," "pretty," or "handsome?" Are you self-conscious or proud about some of your physical features? If so, how does this affect your actions around others?

Do you see yourself as having an advantage because of your physical traits or do you think some of your physical qualities are handicaps? What does being handicapped really mean?

Handicapped often implies any physical or mental condition that restricts a person from optimum performance. Wearing glasses might be viewed as a handicap. But, is it the same as being confined to a wheel chair or experiencing the loss of sight?

Obviously, some physical handicaps can limit performance; however, they need not limit one's self-concept. There are many people who have minor physical disabilities who worry about themselves and what others might think. They develop poor self-concepts which prevent them from having a positive outlook on life and accomplishing things. There are others who have severe physical handicaps whose positive self-concepts inspire others around them.

Cole was an incredible young man who had qualified for his state swimming meet for his high school. One day, he climbed a tree to trim some branches. He accidentally touched a live electric wire which sent thousands of volts through his body. He was near death, but he survived. He was severely burned and his left arm and leg were amputated. His life was altered drastically. He felt unattractive, useless, and unworthy of having close friends. He was depressed and avoided others. He felt his life was ruined and he developed a negative picture of himself.

However, Cole's classmates and friends refused to be rejected and continued to care about him. There was no doubt that Cole's life would be changed forever, but this did not mean that he was also destined to continue thinking negatively about himself. He eventually accepted his new physical self, and with the support of his friends, discovered that he had many strengths.

Cole became a peer facilitator. He studied and practiced many of the skills that are presented in this book. He learned to help others and, in doing so, he learned to like himself even better. He was admired by his peers because of his courage, sense of humor, and resilience. He was open and honest with himself and others. He was a successful small group leader and became a special friend to others at his school. His positive self-concept enabled him to overcome a personal tragedy.

Many things can affect how you see yourself besides gender, race, and physical characteristics; your parents' social position in the community, the clothes you have to wear, activities and sports in which you chose to participate, whether you are on a team or not, your birth order, and your grades in school, for example.

Pause for a minute and see yourself standing in the middle of a gymnasium. You are alone. Think of all the people that have made a positive impact on you and have been instrumental in your success. Picture those people sitting in the bleachers to the left of you. What would you say to them?

Now imagine that sitting in the bleachers to the right of you are some people who have, in their way, affected you in an undesirable way. They have tried to lower your self-concept. Because of them you have had some negative thoughts about yourself. Who is sitting there? What would you say to them?

We realize that many events, people, and things are instrumental in the formation of our self. The question that we may now ask ourselves is, "How do I find out more about myself?"

The process for learning more about who you are is not complicated. First, you can think about it, become introspective, and analyze your behavior, values, and thoughts. You may want to begin by focusing on whether you see yourself as a positive or a negative person. Are you someone who wakes up happy, challenged, ready to go? Or, do you wake up tired, depressed, angry, and ready to confront anyone who gets in your way?

Becoming aware of your self and evaluating your thoughts and ideas is difficult to do alone. There is an old saying, "The eye cannot see the eyeball." Even though you may learn a lot through self-study, eventually you will need the help of others in self-discovery. You need to know how others see you and the kind of impact your actions have on them. You need both their encouragement and their *constructive* criticism.

Self-Disclosure

Self-disclosure is the process of telling someone else something about yourself. It may be something that is quite obvious or it may be a feeling or thought that you have never shared before. It may be something you see as quite ordinary or it may be quite extraordinary. Self-disclosure means revealing something about self. It does not mean, necessarily, sharing deep dark secrets.

The process of self-disclosure might be viewed as twofold. First, you have to talk about yourself. You tell about your feelings, your ideas, and some of the events of your life. This may be an opportunity to "unload" things that you may have been carrying around with you for a long time. Talking about yourself to a willing listener gives you a chance to stand back and look at your "words." This process enables you to understand more of your own thoughts and feelings.

The second part of the process involves gaining a perspective of yourself through another person's eyes. This person is a sounding board-someone to listen to you.

There are some risks involved. The person listening to you may not value the same things you do. That person may not give you the response that you expect. For instance, Missy decided to tell a classmate that she was angry with her friends. "I hate them.... They are talking about me behind my back." She said that they were mad at her because she had secretly dated her best friend's boyfriend. Missy continued, "It's none of their business. I can do what I want, with who I want. Don't you agree?" Missy had self-disclosed. She wanted to get someone else's opinion, or did she?

Another risk of self-disclosure is that the listener may not keep the matter private. For example, Missy's classmate may not feel obligated to keep the information confidential. Picking a person to whom you want to self-disclose is an important matter, especially if you want to learn more about yourself.

Peer facilitators are trained listeners. They do not judge or show disrespect. They work hard at understanding what is being said and at being worthy of the person's trust.

It can be helpful if you are selective about when and where to self-disclose. It is difficult to share personal things over the telephone. You may miss nonverbal communication signals, such as facial expressions, gestures, or body movement. Nevertheless, a lot of people self-disclose information about themselves over the phone. There are many crisis centers that depend upon trained people to facilitate others over the phone. There are hotlines for suicide prevention, runaways, 911—all of which help people self-disclose during emergencies.

People can learn a lot about themselves by self-disclosing in a group. Group members can intensify the experience because there are so many more listeners and helpers. Trained leaders know how to help members self-disclose and can help facilitate them. Sometimes there is a discrepancy in the picture you paint of yourself and the one others see. Is it an OUCH! Or is what you see a YEAH! Your response depends upon the feedback, and more importantly, it depends upon who is sending the feedback.

Stepping back, deciding if you have heard this information before and evaluating if this person really is in a position to evaluate you, is an important step to take. Now the challenge begins. Do you believe it? And if you do believe it, then what is the next step in altering your behavior so as to project a different self-image?

The search for self begins with self-disclosure. This leads to an increased self-awareness. As you become more aware of your strengths and limitations, your needs and goals, your behaviors and its effect on others, you are beginning to form a personal identity. More importantly, the process is likely to help you develop a positive self-image.

Changing the Self

Suppose you discover something about yourself that you would like to change. What can you do? Is it really possible to change who you are? Yes! It may be a slow process, like developing muscles or losing weight. If you want to be good at something, you know you must practice. If you want to develop a new skill, then you must practice. If you want to develop a more positive image of yourself, then you must practice.

There have been many hours, experiences, and people that have contributed to making you who you are. It takes special strategies and new experiences at times to break old habits and achieve new goals.

If you want to change, decide what it is *exactly* that you want to happen. What special traits do you want to develop? For instance, you may want to develop some specific traits that would help you gain closer friendships. One study showed teenage boys tended to prefer male friends who were athletic, honest, responsible, friendly, and who had similar interests. Girls looked for many of the same things in friendships and included humor, kindness, and consideration.

The same study showed that boys did not like peers who caused trouble in school, spent a lot of time seeking attention, were bossy or phony, or who settled matters by fighting. Boys with these characteristics were avoided. Girls reported that they disliked peers who were conceited, unfriendly, acted inappropriately in a given situation, and who took no pride in their appearance.

Four Strategies for Change

Here are four useful strategies that can affect how you see yourself and how others see you.

Strategy 1:
Forget the negative.

Do not absorb all the negative comments about others and about yourself that you may hear. You have to decide which of those comments are meaningful and which are not. You also have to consider the source. Is this a caring and trustworthy person, or is this a person who is insensitive and judgmental?

It is often too easy to focus on the negative. The media floods us daily with news about wars, illness, murders, and social problems. We also know that life is full of conflicts. One study suggested that an elementary school child will likely deal with over 2,000 conflicts during a school year. Some of these will be minor and be resolved quickly. Some will be ignored. Others will be more lasting and even crippling. Dwelling on the negative can be an exercise in futility unless one is willing to take action.

Strategy 2:
Recall the positive.

Focus on the successes and achievements that you have already obtained or experienced. Reinforcing the positive things in life can help you feel good about yourself and give you the courage to

confront other issues. It may be helpful to recall pleasant memories and feelings. Just like your radio, you will occasionally have to listen to stations you do not want to, but continue to turn the dial to your favorite songs. Dialing to positive images will give you the support for dealing with difficult times.

Strategy 3:
Express yourself positively.

As Ralph Waldo Emerson, the noted writer stated, "You become what you think of yourself all day long." People who have the habit of saying, "I can't!" are often caught in a self-fulfilling prophecy. Their attitude only allows them to try halfheartedly. They are thinking defeat before they even start. The energy that they could use to bring about a positive change is being channeled into making excuses. Not too surprisingly, this kind of attitude is not very attractive to others.

Simply changing the tone and content of the statement to, "I can" or "I will" often makes a positive difference. There is a tone of determination and commitment. Likewise, "I can" and "I will" is stronger and more effective than "I ought to" or "I should."

Strategy 4:
Take action.

As the *Nike* commercial said, "Just do it!" This sounds simple, perhaps too simple. However, taking action, even if only a small step, is essential for change.

Instead of complaining about his math test scores, John decided to take a positive approach. He first assessed his math skills and attitudes. He realized that continued griping about the teacher and the nature of the test would not make things better. Now, he was aware that he spent too much time worrying and saying to himself, "I am going to fail this test."

He remembered a time when he did well in math and how he studied. At that time, he was confident and sensed that he would do well. John began reminding himself that he was a good student; he had been successful before and could be again. Instead of saying, "I should study harder for the next test," he said, "I will study harder." And, he did. His first step was to study twenty minutes in the morning before catching the school bus. The results of John's actions were positive, not only did he make a better grade on his math test, but he soon developed a positive self-concept regarding himself and his abilities in math.

Awareness of Others

Our self-concept is so dependent upon relationships with others that an important part of self-development is becoming more aware of others. Our identities depend upon what people say to us and how they react to the things we do and say. Other people play an integral part in how we see ourselves. It makes sense for us to slow down and become more aware of those around us. We need to be aware of their feelings, needs, and interests.

A key ingredient for helping others is being aware of their uniqueness, including their special needs and concerns. This means that you will have to become an attentive listener and observer. Only then can you begin to help them think of ways to solve their problems or make responsible decisions.

Becoming sensitive to others will assist you in becoming a better person yourself. Your efforts to reach out to others will provide you with a sense of personal self-worth. As a peer facilitator, your awareness of others may assist you in helping others in a variety of ways: learning a new skill, sharing religious convictions, listening and referring someone in a time of need-providing you with a true sense of self-worth.

Self as Helper

After increasing your awareness of yourself and others, you are ready to begin helping others. There is tremendous power in people helping people. In times of disaster, we find flood victims receiving clothing, food, and money from people everywhere. One peer facilitator group sorted old clothing and cleaned it for homeless families. In communities every-where, there are people who need help.

In addition to the elements of under-standing, caring, trust, and so forth, some other important qualities in a helping relationship are empathy, respect, warmth, concreteness, genuineness, and self-disclosure. Developing skills in each of these areas will assist you in gaining the necessary components for becoming an excellent peer facilitator.

Empathy is simply the ability to have the depth and understanding related to another person's experience. At times it is difficult to place ourselves in someone else's shoes, but it is a valuable trait. Think about your own parents and a time they have been very angry with you because you did not come home on time. Using empathy, you might have better under-stood their anger and realized they were also concerned about your well-being.

Respect is having a genuine belief in someone else. Friendships need respect and understanding. Warmth is also impor-tant to becoming a helper. Showing love and caring toward another enhances the ability of communicating.

Concreteness is being specific with others about their behavior. As a helper you do not speak in generalities. You would say, "Everyone seems to be using crack, don't you agree?" Instead, you would state your concern concretely, " I have heard you are using crack. Would you like to talk about it with me?"

Genuineness, being honest and real, is essential for a helper. Realizing the person you are talking with is sincere and caring will enhance the relationship. Also, self-disclosure from you will convey to the other person that you may have felt or experienced some of the same feelings or events.

Summary

What you are embarking on in this program is not just the ability to become a peer facilitator. You are also developing the necessary skills for becoming a partner.

Partnerships are those events that pull us together. You will hopefully be involved in many partnerships throughout your life: husband—wife, father—son, mother—daughter, employer—employee, friend—friend, and neighbor—neighbor. The characteristics and traits you are learning now are life skills to provide you with a foundation for developing yourself as a helper and partner in your relationships now and in the future.

If you can make other students feel that you care about what happens to them and help them to have some successes in their lives, they will begin to gain confi-dence in their abilities and form better self-concepts. Accept others as they are, and help them to change as they gain understanding about themselves and their abilities through their own experiences.

Activity 3.1
Lifeline Events

Purpose:

To increase awareness of how some events are benchmarks in people's lives.

Materials:

Paper and pencils

Procedures:

1. On a piece of paper, draw a straight horizontal line. The line is then divided into three equal parts.

2. At the left end of the line, write the date of your birthday. Write today's date on the right end of the line.

3. Think of three important events which occurred in your life during elementary school. Going from left to right on your time-line, in chronological order, draw three symbols or pictures which represent these three events. Record these in the first section of the time-line.

4. Next, think of three significant events which occurred in junior high or middle school. Record them in the second section of your lifeline by using symbols or pictures.

5. Finally, pick one event which has occurred within the past year which has had an important effect on your life. Mark it on your lifeline.

6. Get into a group of three. The individuals in turn share one event from each section on their time-lines. Group members share only those events which they want to talk about.

Key Questions:

What kinds of feelings—pleasant, unpleasant, or both—were associated with the different events? What feelings or events were similar among group members? How much control did you have over the events happening? How much control do you have over how you feel about the events now? What is one event you would like to be able to record on your time-line this year? In the next five years? And, sometime in your life-time?

Activity 3.2
Presenting ME

Purpose:

To increase self-awareness

Materials:

Paper, magazines, scissors, glue

Procedures:

1. Using letters or pictures from old magazines, newspapers, or other sources, find samples of things which represent you.

2. Cut and paste the letters, pictures, symbols, and so forth to create a "ME Presentation" about yourself.

3. In small groups or before the entire class, present your ME poster. Tell some of the reasons you selected certain pictures and the image you were trying to create.

4. After you have shared your "ME Presentation," give others in the group or class a chance to tell their reactions. What would they have added? What surprised them, if anything?

Key Questions:

What outside or easily observable qualities did people present? Which private or internal qualities were presented? Do you always send the same ME message to people? Is it the same to everyone or how is it different? What are some other ways in which you can present yourself to others?

Chapter 4

Attentive Listening and Observing

Most of us love to talk, especially if it is about ourselves. Telling others about the events in our lives, our thoughts, and opinions; what we have observed; and how we feel can be a satisfying personal experience. It makes us feel a part of the world, especially if someone is listening to us.

Some people find talking to be so fascinating and pleasurable that it makes no difference whether anyone is listening carefully or not. They just talk... and talk... and talk. It makes them feel important. It gives them a sense of being unique and alive.

Words play a big part in our lives. They may be spoken aloud or thought silently. Even if people do not say a lot when they are with others, it is impossible for them to remain silent within themselves. Self-talk goes on. Our unspoken words and reactions to what others say and do are a part of our thinking process. Eventually, however, talk must serve some purpose other than thinking. It must also go beyond saying something simply to express ourselves and to gain attention. Talking with others and sharing ideas enables us to relate to people. We are then able to develop healthy interpersonal relationships.

Talking with others is probably the most obvious form of communication. It seems that the words we use and the meaning that we try to give them are the focus of our interactions. Yet, there are other forms of communication. There are nonverbal messages being sent and received. Various meanings are attached to them. We communicate with gestures, movements, and the tones of our voice as well as the choice of our words.

It is not easy to describe how communication works. Some scholars have outlined the sequence of events where a person thinks of a message, sends it, and then someone else receives it. In addition, the senders and receivers are involved in the process of seeing, hearing, interpreting, concluding, and reacting. It is a complicated process that we often take for granted. It is also the source of a lot of misunderstanding and personal problems.

Many of the problems that people face in everyday life are a result of poor communication skills. Conflicts come about when people cannot read or hear the other person and there is a lack of communication. Conflicts also result when message senders communicate an attitude which makes it difficult to hear accurate messages. Think of how many different ways that you can say, "That was really neat?" The tone of your voice, the emphasis on certain words, and your gestures can communicate different meanings.

Interpersonal relationships are based on communication, for better or for worse. When communication skills are poor, relationships between people tend to struggle. They are less satisfying and sometimes avoided. When communication is effective, there is more pleasure in being together and sharing experiences. When there are communication barriers, defensiveness prevents accurate messages from being sent or received. Interpersonal relationships are enhanced or broken down because of the way we talk to and with others. It follows, then, that part of helping another person is learning how to communicate.

Although the helping process is more than just talking, the words that we use and the way we communicate is a good place to start. What you say and do as a peer facilitator will make a difference in the way your relationships develop and the kind of help that you can give. Perhaps more importantly, it will also determine the kind of helping role that someone will want you to play. The person's responsiveness to your desire to help depends on communication skills.

Communication Skills

We know that human beings are not born knowing how to communicate with others. Interpersonal skills are learned just as so many other life skills. We first learn how to communicate from our parents and caretakers when we are infants and small children. We watch and listen. We try out what we see and hear, sometimes with mixed results. If we are lucky, our parents and teachers, and the other significant people in our lives, have modeled for us the very best of communications skills and have given us a chance to practice with them.

We can improve our communications skills by first understanding their value and seeing a need to learn them. When we recognize that certain things we do can either open or close communication, then we begin to think of ways to improve our relationships. We can identify those that we want to use more often in helping relationships. We can practice those that seem to be the most facilitative. Some skills are learned at a faster pace than others, but most take time and practice to master. As we make more progress, the skills become easier to use and manage. They become a natural part of the way in which we communicate with others.

The more you use a skill, the more natural it will feel. In that sense, it is no different than learning to play tennis for the first time and hitting with a backhand stroke. While learning the stroke, you may feel awkward and uncomfortable. You may even feel self-conscious, especially when you repeatedly miss the ball or hit it into the net. You may think of giving up, or changing your approach to something that feels more natural.

This is where coaches, or friends who are also taking lessons, can play important roles. They can watch and practice with you. They can encourage you by taking note of your progress or help you spot little habits which keep you from getting better. They can draw your attention to the little things that make a difference between success and failure. The value of slowing the game down, isolating certain parts that need drill, and working to put combinations of skills in place are the same in peer facilitator work as they are in learning other things, such as tennis.

This chapter is designed to increase your awareness about the need for interpersonal communication skills and to present some ideas about the most basic skill of all—listening. In the next chapter you will learn more about how to respond to others, using six high facilitative skills. They are a part of our "facilitative model." We will also look at some other responses that tend to be less facilitative, but that may, at times, be useful.

As in most things that require a set of skills to be successful, there are some things that you can do to get ready. You can put yourself in a good position to hit a ball, type a letter, play a piano, or cast a fishing line, and probably increase your chances of success, if you know how.

Likewise, you can put yourself in a position so that you can get ready to hear others and to respond to them after they have shared ideas with you. In that respect, it is the same as assuming a set or stance to get ready to hit a back-stroke in tennis. The set or stance simply increases the chances that you will be more successful. It does not mean that you will hit the ball every time or that you will always make good contact. But, you will be better prepared.

You will be taking part in some learning exercises during your training and preparation to be a peer facilitator. It is up to you to make the best use of what you experience in those exercises, to practice and master the basic skills, and then to apply them in other situations. You will be responsible for evaluating your own progress and work. You, along with your friends, will want to discover those things about yourself which get in the way of effectively communicating with others and to make some changes. You will also be looking for your strengths which add to your skill development and can become a part of your helping style.

Eventually, the communication and interpersonal skills that you will learn will feel natural. They will be a part of your style and you will be glad to have developed and discovered a new part of yourself that you can enjoy the rest of your life.

The Art of Listening

Before you can send a response to someone, you must first listen to them. Since you spend so much of your time listening to your parents, teachers, and friends, this basic communication skill may seem like a simple thing to do. "I've been listening to people all my life," you may say.

Careful and attentive listening, however, is different than casual talk. It is listening with a focus, with a purpose of trying to communicate. Unfortunately, too much of the time communication is a one-way street, where the person talking assumes that the person who is listening is hearing everything that is said and is hearing it accurately.

Careful and attentive listening is more than being quiet while others are talking. It is more than giving them the courtesy to talk about things that are of interest to them. It is more than giving them a chance to voice their opinions or tell about events in their lives. When listening attentively and carefully, you concentrate on the words that are being said, the feelings that go with the words, and the behaviors that go with those feelings and words. You are trying to get the message, to really read the person. Because there are so few attentive and careful listeners in most people's daily lives, people are often surprised to learn that they communicate many messages. They are trying to say what is on their mind, but they also communicate a lot more about themselves, their values, their attitudes, and their willingness to share their ideas.

Four Steps to Careful Listening

There are four steps to careful listening. Of course, in order to be a good listener, you must also attend to the person's words and behaviors. The four steps are: 1) Look at the person who is talking; 2) Pay attention to the words that the person is using; 3) Listen and look for the feelings that go with the words; and, 4) Say something to show that you have heard the person. Let us take a closer look at these four steps.

1. *Look at the person who is talking.*

When you are trying to facilitate another person to talk with you, begin by getting yourself in a comfortable and relaxed position. Position yourself so that you can see the person's face and have some eye contact. Look at the person. This invites that person to talk and lets the person know that you are an interested and willing listener.

Although you could probably hear the person's words if you turned your back, you would not be able to communicate as well. This has been demonstrated many times in different experimental studies. When you cannot see the person, too many communication clues are missed and the person may wonder if you care about what is being said. Have you ever talked with others on the telephone and wondered how they were reacting to what you were saying? You can give them the benefit of the doubt that they are listening to you and continue talking, when in fact

they may be reading a book, watching television, or making gestures to someone else in the room. They may be distracted, but you would not know it.

Have you ever found yourself trying to strike up a conversation with people who are doing something besides looking at you. Maybe they are reading a magazine or the paper, watching television, preparing dinner, or doing homework. Even though they may be listening to your words, if they do not look at you there is something lost in the communication. You have to work harder and you are not encouraged to talk about matters in depth. Effective communication is a two-way street that involves people looking at each other.

When you, as a listener, are in the same room and looking at the person who is talking to you, you want to hear what is being said. Your body posture, facial expressions, and eyes send the message that you are being attentive. We will talk about nonverbal communication later, but it is clear that looking at the person is the first step to being a good facilitator of communication.

2. Pay attention to the words.

Now that the person is talking, you must listen to the words that are being said. Take note of them and try to avoid drifting away into your own thoughts. What the person says may stimulate you to think about situations in your own life and make you lose your concentration. If this happens, you will miss out on some things and may lose the flow of the topic or conversation. One rather poor listener kept saying, "What was that again?"

The people who are talking to you are doing the best that they can to tell their stories. They use words that describe events or ideas. They are sharing their personal perspectives or points of views with you. Sometimes a particular choice of words conveys what they are really experiencing and thinking. Here are three people talking about similar situations.

Person one: "My old man is a jerk. He expects me to give him everything that I earn in my part time job. I don't make much, but he is always on my case about not paying my way and that I'm old enough to fork up some money for the family. It causes us to fight a lot."

Person two: "My dad is something else, at times. He wants me to give him the money I earn in my part time job. He says that I'm old enough to make my own way and part of that is giving him money for family expenses. It makes us argue a lot."

Person three: "My dad puts a lot of pressure on me. He says that I should give him the money from my part time job. He wants me to pay part of the family expenses. Even though I'm older now, it is still disappointing to think he wants it all. It causes a lot of conflict between us."

Even though these three situations are similar because of the events and issue involved, there is, nevertheless, something different about each one. What is the difference to you? What is communicated about the fathers? What is being said by the person who is talking about the father?

When a person is talking with you, it can be helpful to string together some of the ideas and look for a common theme among them. How are the ideas related? What are the main ones being expressed? If you were asked to summarize the most important points that each person made, what would you say?

Robert D. Myrick and Betsy E. Folk

3. *Be aware of the feelings that go with the words.*

You cannot talk without a feeling. You may try to disguise your feelings, but eventually what you are experiencing will come out. Our emotions always accompany our ideas.

When you are first starting to be a helper, you may listen only to the words of the story. You may be so interested in the events or ideas that you miss the feelings being communicated.

One way to help you to listen for feelings, of course, is to ask yourself, "Am I hearing *pleasant* or *unpleasant* feelings, or *both*?" It can be helpful if you develop your feeling word vocabulary. Look at the lists of feeling words on the following page. Notice the different words that describe feelings. Which of these are familiar to you? Which words express the right shade of meaning that you have experienced?

As you look at the feeling words lists , think of some situations where such words might capture what you or someone else might be experiencing. For example, imagine that Jeremy, a friend of yours, has just been told that his friendly and kind grandfather died unexpectedly.

In this case, it might be easy to hypothesize that some unpleasant feelings might be present (e.g. cheated, confused, crushed, at a loss, grief, lonely, hurt, sad, shocked, sorrowful, stunned, tearful). You would have to listen to Jeremy talk about his grandfather to help you to decide which of these words might best describe his feelings. Or, you may need to add some other unpleasant feeling words that are not on the list.

Because Jeremy loved and cared for his grandfather, is it possible that even in sorrow and sadness there might also be some pleasant feelings expressed? Would you also be able to hear and acknowledge those (e.g. warm, cared, enjoyed, proud, grateful, honored, impressed, inspired)?

Listening for pleasant and unpleasant feelings can give you clues as to what others are experiencing. These experiences may have been a part of the past. For example, "My grandfather told such funny stories and played all kinds of games with us," may suggest that in the past pleasant feelings (e.g. enjoyed, fun, challenged, enchanted, excited, or fascinated) were a part of being around his grandfather. "He was a wonderful person and everyone loved him. I can't believe that I'll no longer be able to listen to his stories."

In this instance, there may be some pleasant and unpleasant feelings that are evident as Jeremy talks. Those feelings are now in the present. They are immediate. Can you think of some? What might Jeremy be feeling now if he were talking with you? You might say, "You talk about your grandfather with a great deal of pride and it hurts to think that you won't hear any more of his stories."

Before you can respond, of course, you must first hear what the person is saying and be aware of what the person is experiencing. Effective helpers are good listeners. They come to sense what the person is experiencing, going beyond the words at times to grasp the emotions. Feelings are always there in a conversation or interview and they should not be ignored or dismissed as unimportant.

Unpleasant Feelings Words

Abandoned	Distraught	Left Out	Sad
Agony	Disturbed	Lonely	Scared
Ambivalent	Dominated	Longing	Shocked
Angry	Divided	Low	Skeptical
Annoyed	Dubious	Mad	Sorrowful
Anxious	Empty	Maudlin	Startled
Betrayed	Envious	Mean	Strained
Bitter	Exasperated	Melancholy	Stupid
Bored	Exhausted	Miserable	Stunned
Burdened	Fatigued	Nervous	Tenuous
Cheated	Fearful	Odd	Tense
Cold	Flustered	Overwhelmed	Threatened
Condemned	Foolish	Pain	Tired
Confused	Frantic	Panicked	Trapped
Crushed	Frustrated	Persecuted	Troubled
Defeated	Frightened	Petrified	Uneasy
Despair	Grief	Pity	Unsettled
Destructive	Guilty	Pressured	Vulnerable
Different	Intimidated	Quarrelsome	Weak
Diminished	Irritated	Rejected	Weepy
Discontented	Isolated	Remorse	Worried
Distracted	Jealous	Restless	

Pleasant Feeling Words

Adequate	Delighted	Generous	Loved
Affectionate	Determined	Glad	Peaceful
Befriended	Eager	Gratified	Pleasant
Bold	Ecstatic	Groovy	Pleased
Calm	Enchanted	Happy	Proud
Capable	Enhanced	Helpful	Refreshed
Caring	Energetic	High	Relaxed
Challenged	Enervated	Honored	Relieved
Charmed	Enjoyed	Important	Rewarded
Cheerful	Excited	Impressed	Safe
Clever	Fascinated	Infatuated	Satisfied
Comforting	Fearless	Inspired	Secure
Confident	Free	Joyful	Settled
Content	Fulfilled	Kind	Sure
		Loving	Warm

Robert D. Myrick and Betsy E. Folk

4. *Say something to show that you have been listening.*

Now it is time for you to do something, to say something, to show that you have been an attentive and careful listener. It is seldom helpful to let a person ramble on, talking about a number of different events or ideas. It is not enough to say, "I know what you mean;" or "I understand." While these kinds of statements are well intended, they fail to show understanding or that you really heard what was said or felt.

Attentive and careful listeners will have something to say when it is their turn to talk. First, they will not change the subject, unless they know that they deliberately want to redirect the conversation to a different topic. Second, they do not always wait until the person has told all of the story before making a response. If a person is telling the story in great detail, sharing a lot of information at one time, you may have to interrupt and make a response that suggests that you are following along and that you are being a careful listener.

Look at the following example:

Nathan: "I would like to be able to have my own band someday. A bunch of us get together and make music. I play lead guitar, but we need a singer. I'm probably just dreaming."

Peer Helper: "You have fun playing your guitar and the thought of having your own band is really an exciting idea."

Nathan: "Yeah. It would great to be on stage, to have an audience., but...."

Peer Helper: "You'd enjoy performing for others. But, then you seem uncertain whether that could ever happen."

Nathan: "I know our group is good, but we'd have to practice more. You know, to form a band isn't easy. I'm not even sure whether the rest of the guys would be interested or would practice and make a go of it."

Peer Helper: "So right now this is your idea and something you haven't yet talked to the group about. It would be a lot of hard work and you seem unsure."

Nathan: "Well, I guess I could talk with them about it the next time we act together. I know some of them have to be thinking the same thing too. We are really good. It even surprised me."

Peer Helper: "What would you say to them about it?"

In this example, the peer helper used feeling words in statements to show that Nathan's feelings had been heard as well as his ideas. It appeared that Nathan was *uncertain* about what was needed to form a band and whether that was a next step or not. He seemed *proud* of the group's efforts, but was *skeptical* about taking action to form a band. Getting him to think about what he might say to the group encouraged him to explore the idea further.

You will also note that the peer helper did not offer an opinion or make any kind of judgment. No advice was given. Even though some encouraging remarks might be made, the peer helper is trying to be a good listener by following the ideas and tuning into the feelings that were expressed by Nathan. This has a way of encouraging Nathan to talk more, to explore more, and to discover what he might want to do.

It is a special experience to talk with people who can restrain themselves long enough to give you a chance to think about something in depth. The person is giving us a gift, the gift of being an attentive listener and giving us the luxury of talking about ourselves, our ideas, and feelings. When that person knows how to facilitate us in our talking and sharing, they provide us a rich and rewarding experience.

The Art of Observing

Being an effective facilitator involves listening and observing. You have probably heard the expression, "Action speaks louder than words." Interestingly enough, this is also true in the helping process. First, people express themselves nonverbally as well as verbally and, second, getting a person to take responsible action is better than just talking a subject to death.

Some researchers claim that our nonverbal behaviors play the biggest part in our communication with others. One study suggested that in a typical two-person conversation, less than 35% of the messages or meanings are conveyed through words. About 65% of the communication is nonverbal.

In other words, we communicate through the way in which we dress, stand or sit, gesture, use facial expressions, direct our eyes, or position ourselves in a space.

In addition, our tone of voice, pauses, rate of speech, and emphasis on words give clues to what we are thinking, feeling, and trying to communicate. Our nonverbal behaviors send messages. Sometimes they are consistent with our words, which makes understanding much easier. Sometimes they are inconsistent, which is confusing or puzzling. At other times, they provide us with mixed messages, emphasizing how complex the topics or issues being discussed may be.

Peer facilitators know that a smile and calm voice communicates friendliness and acceptance. Facing the person directly in a relaxed posture usually says that you are ready to listen or to be involved. Learning forward to some degree may suggest that the listener is open and available, where leaning back, perhaps in a slouch, may say, "I'm bored" or "I'm too tired to be talking about this now." Of course, steady eye contact is typical for people in our society who are deep in conversation. Staring is a different matter and can make people uncomfortable and defensive. In general, we know that there is more eye contact between people who like each other.

When you are working as a peer facilitator, the persons you are helping will always be communicating something through their body and tone of voice. You will want to become aware of that kind of communication and use it in your work. At the same time, you will also be sending messages through your own body and tone of voice.

Likewise, it will be helpful to be aware of what you are experiencing. If you find yourself getting tense and impatient, your body may be sending out the message,

"I'm anxious and frustrated." The intensity of this message may determine whether or not the person will want to continue talking. Therefore, you will keep an eye on your own behaviors as well as those of others.

Although we can never be sure what others are experiencing (feeling), we can be observant of nonverbal behavior and attempt to understand it. You may sense that others are insincere, even though they are trying to convince you otherwise. What clues give you this impression? You may note that people say one thing but do not act accordingly. They may be giving double messages and they may not even be aware of it themselves.

There are no encyclopedias or dictionaries that explain nonverbal behaviors. A few authors have tried to interpret the meaning of people's actions, but nonverbal messages are usually too ambiguous to give us much confidence in universal interpretations. Some behaviors as messages are easy to interpret because they are so obvious and so often related to a certain experience.

A parent who is shaking a finger at a small child and using a harsh voice is issuing a threat or warning and giving direction. There is probably a firmness in the voice that could be viewed as demanding or, perhaps, even demeaning. How that message is received by the child may depend on the words that went with the actions and past experiences with such behavior, but the unpleasantness is usually clear.

Another problem with interpreting nonverbal behavior is that actions can be used to communicate many kinds of feelings. Anger, for instance, might be expressed through a hostile voice, a pounding of a fist, or by throwing something across a room. Anger may also be expressed by tears, or perhaps through a more quiet means such as a squinting of the eyes or a silent withdrawal from participation. Happiness can be expressed through loud laughter and smiles, or it may be shown through tears or a stunned silence.

There are also differences among cultural groups, where some behaviors communicate special meanings that a different social group may not understand or may misinterpret. Therefore, while we must be observant and take note of nonverbal behaviors to help us communicate, verbal language by comparison is less limited and can become a more powerful tool to communicate.

Summary

We know that our feelings are communicated more through our nonverbal than our verbal behavior. Our nonverbal messages are probably more powerful than our verbal ones, but they are also less precise and difficult to interpret accurately. The best communication between people involves both verbal and nonverbal ways of expressing one's self. The more that they are in harmony or congruent with each other, the easier it is to follow and understand what is being communicated. Therefore, attentive listening and observing are peer facilitator skills that must be learned and practiced.

Activity 4.1
Twisting the Feelings

Purpose:

To illustrate the importance of how something is said, as well as what is said.

Materials:

List of Feeling Words and the Woodchuck Tongue Twister (Optional: Other tongue twist sayings).

Procedures:

1. Look at the following tongue twister.

   "How much wood could a woodchuck chuck, if a woodchuck could chuck wood?"

2. Pick one of the feeling words from Table 4.1 and write it on a card or piece of paper.

3. Put the cards or paper in a random pile on a table in front of the room.

4. Taking turns, one student at a time draws a feeling word and then recites the tongue twister using the feeling word to determine the inflection. How would a person with that feeling say the tongue twister? How might they act as they are saying it?

5. After finishing the twister, ask others in the class to guess the feeling word. If necessary, repeat the twister and feeling one more time.

6. After everyone has had a turn, discuss the clues which helped identify the feelings.

Key Questions:

What body language did you notice which helped (or detracted) from the feeling which was being communicated.? Which feeling words were the easiest to guess? Why is it important to listen for the feelings that go with the words that a person is speaking? Is it possible to cover up feelings with words?

Robert D. Myrick and Betsy E. Folk

Activity 4.2
The Video Machine Game

Purpose:

To practice listening and observing skills.

Materials:

The Video Machine Direction Cards:

1 **Play:** The Machine and Talker start.

2. **Stop:** The Machine and Talker stop immediately.

3. **Pause:** The Machine states the Talker's current feelings (here and now).

4. **Reverse/Playback:** The Machine reenacts (imitates) words and movements of what the Talker has already presented.

5. **Fast Forward:** The Machine tries to guess what the Talker is going to do or say next.

6. **Eject:** The Machine makes a final summary statement and everyone stops.

Procedures:

1. In a group of three, each person is given one of three roles: a) The Talker; b) The Video Machine; c) The Operator

2. The Talker sits across from the Machine who is listening and recording in memory what is being said. The Operator, using the direction cards listed above, will "play" a card. The Talker stops while the Machine responds by following the appropriate directions. For example, the Operator may play the STOP card and then play the REVERSE/PLAYBACK card, in which case the Talker stops and the Machine acts out the body language and tries to repeat the words used by the Talker. The Operator then uses the PLAY card to start action again, as the Talker continues.

3. Each person in a triad takes a turn as Talker, Machine, and Operator in three different 5- to 7-minute rounds.

4. The first Talker chooses one of the topics below and begins telling the Machine related ideas and thoughts. The Machine listens attentively. The Operator, in short intervals, displays the different cards. The Machine follows the directions for each card.

5. When the Operator plays the EJECT card, the Machine makes a final summary statement and then, roles are changed, a new topic is selected, and the game begins again with the new Operator.

6. Players rotate the roles until all three have played each role. Then, talk together about the experience. Topics for the *Video Machine Game:*

   A. Ways to Win Friends and Influence People

   B. The Good and the Bad about Television

   C. Censoring Music, TV, Films, and Books

   D. Things I Would Hate to Fail

   E. My Fears and Hopes about the Future

   F. What Parents Don't Understand About Teenagers

Key Questions:

How do the cards reflect communication skills used by a helping person? When you were the machine, was it easier to act on the PAUSE, REVERSE/PLAYBACK, or FAST FORWARD cards? Which was the most difficult? Can you think of times when people have, in their own way, held up these kinds of cards for you? How did these directions make you feel and act? What other cards do people hold up to talkers? Do such messages help or hinder communication?

Robert D. Myrick and Betsy E. Folk

Chapter 5

The Art of Responding

Once you have observed another person and listened carefully to that person's words, what do you say? It is your turn to respond. What can you do to help the person to continue talking and exploring an idea? How can you be facilitative?

Although we recognize the importance of nonverbal communication and the part that it can play in a helper's role, in this chapter we will give special attention to what a facilitator might say—how you respond and talk with someone can make a difference.

As a peer facilitator, you will rarely, if ever, give memorized speeches or deliver canned words of wisdom while working with others. It is not your job to lecture others or to sit in judgment of them. Rather, your task is to facilitate them to talk about the events in their lives and what they are thinking and feeling. You want to give them opportunities to explore situations, examine consequences and alternatives, and to consider responsible actions. On occasion, you may have some suggestions for them to add to their list of possible next steps and, in some instances, you will want to guide them to sources of information or resource people.

High Facilitative Responses

There may not be one single best way to organize your thinking in terms of how to respond to others. However, there are six high facilitative responses that lay the foundation of all peer facilitator work and you can learn them. View them as skills to be mastered and use them in your work. If you can master these basic skills, you are in a position to be a very successful helper.

The six high facilitative responses are: **1) feeling-focused responses; 2) clarifying or summarizing responses; 3) open questions; 4) facilitative feedback, as compliments or confrontations; 5) simple acknowledgment; and, 6) linking.** Let us look at each of these in more detail.

The feeling-focused response

It is important to communicate that you understand what a person is experiencing. Demonstrating understanding, as well as some of the other helping conditions, enhances the helping relationship and encourages a person to talk and think more. The feeling-focused response is perhaps the single best response in communicating understanding, since it gives attention to a person's feelings.

When you listen to people talk, you are asking yourself, "Am I hearing *pleasant* feelings, *unpleasant* feelings, or *both*?" You are trying to grasp the essence of what they are experiencing. Here are some examples of feeling-focused responses:

"You seem so excited, Amy"

"John, you're disappointed."

"It makes you sad to think about it."

"You're not sure what to do next."

"You are feeling more relaxed now."

Close examination of these statements will show that each has one important word that makes it a feeling-focused response. That word, of course, is a *feeling* word. It is a word that focuses on what the speaker is personally experiencing, whether pleasant or unpleasant in nature.

Making a feeling-focused response shows that you are a sensitive person, someone who is trying to understand in an empathic sort of way. Such a response also communicates that you are an attentive listener and that you care about what the person is experiencing. More than any other response, it tells a person that you are an understanding, accepting, and respecting helper.

Recognizing and responding to a person's feelings is an essential part of the helping process, but it is not always understood or accepted by critics. There are a few people who believe that feelings are a private matter and should never be discussed. They fear that feelings are so personal that to respond to them is an invasion of privacy, or that attention to feelings is too intimate. They discourage people from sharing feelings, worrying that such self-disclosures reflect unfavorably on people. To the contrary, many of the problems that people face as part of their lives are because they are unaware of how feelings and behaviors are related. Repressing or denying feelings, or what a person is experiencing, sets the stage for the development of personal dysfunctioning and ineffective problem solving. Decision making is clouded and there is a tendency to reject responsibility for our ideas and actions.

Most people are not aware of what they are feeling in situations. Sometimes their feelings are mixed and they are unaware of how those feelings affect their behaviors. At other times, feelings are in conflict with what people believe or would like to believe and may be disguised or hidden. It takes an alert and careful listener to help increase awareness. As awareness increases, one's ability to understand more about self and to make responsible decisions also increases.

To begin a sentence with "You feel..." does not necessarily mean that you are going to respond to a person's feelings. If you were to say, "You feel that the student council president is doing a good job." This would be a statement of what the person *thinks* not feels. It is the person's judgment or idea, rather than what is being experienced. In contrast, you might say, "You are *satisfied*, even *optimistic*, with the president's work." In this case, there are two feeling words which might show personal understanding.

You should also be cautious about giving advice or your own opinion when using the expression, "I feel...." "I feel that you should talk with the teacher" is a statement expressing your own values and ideas. It tells what you think the person should do. It ignores what the person is experiencing and is likely to be less facilitative. Of course, you need to be observant and look for nonverbal cues which suggest what the person has experienced or is experiencing. Taking note of the person's behaviors and searching a feelings word list to describe what you are seeing and hearing is the first step in being a facilitator.

The skill of hearing and responding to a person's feelings takes practice. You may find it difficult to do at first, especially if your feeling word vocabulary is limited. Think of places and situations which involve your peers, perhaps the classroom, at sporting events, in the cafeteria, or in the mall. Imagine the kinds of conversations that take place there. What kinds of feelings are likely to be a part of certain topics?

Be careful not to project your own feelings on people. That is, tune into what they are experiencing rather than what you are experiencing or would have experienced in a similar situation. You may ask yourself, "What would I feel *if* I were in that situation?" These are attempts to "put yourself in another person's shoes." But, this can lead you to talk about your own feelings rather than others. What you might experience could be different, depending on a lot of circumstances. What makes one person mad could make another sad, or even amused. Following the lead of the person you are helping might best be done by asking, "Am I hearing *pleasant, unpleasant,* or *both* kinds of feelings?" Select the one or two best feeling words and try to say something to show that you understand.

One advantage of making a feeling-focused response is that you always get credit for trying to be an understanding, caring, accepting helper. If you are inaccurate, the person will be moved to correct you and align your perceptions. Naturally, you would like to find the most accurate feeling word and reflect it back to the person you are helping. It is pleasing to know that you have captured the moment.

Accurate empathy is something to aim for, but there are many kinds of pleasant and unpleasant feelings. Some are similar, perhaps with a slightly different shade of meaning, and may be more acceptable if not accurate. Feeling mad, for example, can also be reflected as feeling irritated, annoyed, angry, frustrated, and so forth. Your task is to select the best word that shows understanding of what the person is experiencing in a given situation.

The clarifying or summarizing response

As you are listening, you might also be asking yourself, "What are the points that this person is trying to make?" Or, "What are the key events or issues?" This involves taking note of the content or subject.

A clarifying or summarizing response focuses on the main ideas or events. It has a way of centering the conversation, drawing attention to the central ideas or themes. For instance,

"You have decided to practice the piano before school."

"Then you and your parents agree about your going into the military service after graduation."

"At this point, then, you haven't talked with the teacher."

"You are going to get an after-school job first, save your money, and eventually buy your own motorcycle."

A clarifying or summarizing response usually requires the use of fresh words and it attempts to simplify what has been said. It is not the same as parroting or mimicking. Some have called it paraphrasing. These responses highlight a few events or thoughts.

As you may know, when most people talk, they share many ideas at the same time. They may start out talking about one thing, but in the course of talking they are stimulated by another idea which leads them to talk about something else. And, this can go on and on. Fluid talkers can flood us with many ideas, if we let them. They often need help in slowing down and focusing their thoughts and feelings. Inserting a clarifying or summarizing response now and then can be facilitative.

It is useful to make a clarifying or summarizing response when you are unsure if you are following the person's train of thought or if you want to deliberately emphasize something that was said. These statements focus on the content of what was shared with you, rather than the feelings. Both story and feelings are always there and you can have the option of responding to one or to the other. Clarifying responses can be comforting and reassuring to the person you are trying to help.

Lead-in phrases can give you a start. Here are a few examples of lead-ins to clarifying responses:

"You seem to be saying...."

"From what you've said, it seems that...."

"If I'm following you, you're thinking that...."

"In other words, you...."

"Let's see if I understand you, you said...."

"Correct me if I'm wrong, but you're saying...."

"One of the most important ideas that seems to be coming out of what you've been saying is...."

A summarizing statement is similar in that it too focuses on the content of the story, particular events or ideas, or basic themes, but highlights more than one. Here are a few common lead-ins to summarizing responses:

"Okay, at this point, you said... and... and...."

"Up to now I've heard two things. First,.... Second,...."

"You've mentioned several things. Let me see if I can summarize what I've heard thus far. 1... 2... 3...."

"What keeps coming through to me are these ideas, ..."

On occasion you may even interrupt people to clarify or summarize the points that they have shared to that point. This not only lets them know that you are trying to be a good listener and following along, but it helps them to stay focused, to keep from rambling. Likewise, you can also interrupt with a timely feeling-focused response, as discussed earlier. It is not rude to interrupt when your intent to is let the person know that you are listening and want to make sure that you are understanding.

Imagine that you are listening to Daniel, who is saying...

"School is such a bore. The teachers here don't care about me, in fact I know Mr. Hanson is glad that I'm out of his class right now. He's always on my case to get my work in, to study harder. I could do better. But, if I say one little thing in class, he hollers at me and says I should get out and stay out until I shape up. I don't know. Maybe I should see about getting a better job and just quit school. I think I could get a job down at the shop."

It may be perfectly acceptable to let Daniel just talk, to vent his feelings and to ramble on with his ideas. He may need a patient listener who will not interrupt his flow of ideas. What would you say to Daniel? He has paused for a moment and is looking at you. He wants you to say something.

If you are like most friends and casual listeners, you will have a tendency to forget what was said at first and make a response to the last thing that was said. "So, you think a job at the shop would be possible;" or, "You seem hopeful about getting a job." Both of these responses would be considered facilitative, one focusing on feelings and the other clarifying an idea. However, look at what else was said. What feelings were *not* responded to? What ideas might merit more attention? Where would you like to insert some other feeling-focused responses? Some clarifying or summarizing responses?

There will be occasions like this when you will need to use your best judgment as to when to make a facilitative response.

Open questions

It's hard to imagine a conversation without questions being asked. Questions have a way of encouraging sharing, but not all of them are the same. Some are more facilitative than others. Let us look at two kinds: *closed* and *open*.

The *closed* question can be answered briefly, usually with a "yes" or "no." Although closed questions might be enough to get some people to talk openly, they generally require only a few words to answer. They give the impression that you are only interested in quick facts and answers. Sometimes these questions, when given in rapid fashion, can create the image of a detective who is grilling a suspect.

"Do you like English?"

"Did you do your homework?"

"Are you going to the party?"

"Does she always argue with you?"

No matter the subject, closed questions are limiting. They can, on occasion, be useful and practical, especially when you are in a hurry to get a short answer or to confirm something that the person has done or is intending to do.

Open questions, on the other hand, encourage the person to give more details and to respond with more expansive answers. They invite the person to share more. Look at these examples:

"What do you dislike about English?"

"How is your homework going?"

"What are your plans for the party?"

"How does she talk to you?"

You might even contrast these open questions with the closed questions cited above. Can you see any differences? (A closed question) What differences do you notice? (An open question).

How would you feel if the questions were directed to you? What kinds of answers might be possible? What kind of impact do you think such questions might make on others who you are trying to facilitate? Which ones strike you as the most facilitative, ones that would encourage a person to self-disclose and explore ideas more?

In general, questions that begin with *what* or *how* are most facilitative. They are the most productive when judged on how much information a person will share. They make a facilitator's work easier. You will want to increase the use of what and how questions in your work, then look for opportunities to clarify or summarize the answers or focus on the feelings that were behind the words.

This might also be a good place to caution you about the use of the "Why" question. It, too, is an open question. It calls for more information and sharing than a closed question. But, it has some limitations.

Questions that begin with *why* tend to cause people to be defensive. Such questions press people to explain themselves, to be accountable, or to justify. Certainly, the "why" question can be an appropriate challenge at times, but when asked too early or too often in a helping relationship, it may not be facilitative.

Most of us have grown up knowing that not all "why" questions are really questions. They are often forms of advice. Look at the following:

"Why do you play your music so loud?"

"Why don't you do your homework?"

"Why are you always late for class?"

"Why can't you get to work on time?"

There may be a logical explanation for each of the questions and a person answering them may be able to provide us with a logical explanation. However, more often than not, the person will see them as advice. These kinds of questions are used frequently to tell people what to do: turn down the music, do your homework, do not be late to class, and get to work on time.

Most people really do not know how to answer the why question, even when it is truly meant as a question. A what or how question may accomplish the same thing, but be more facilitative. Compare and contrast the following:

"Why do you like him as a friend?"

"What do you see in him as a friend?"

"Do you like him as a friend?"

"Why aren't you going to try out?"

"What's keeping you from trying out?"

"You're not going to try out, are you?"

"Why don't you like the class?

"How would you describe the class?"

"Did you think that it was a good or bad class?"

As a peer facilitator, you want people to talk with you about their ideas and feelings. You will be asking them questions to help them think more specifically about whatever topic is being discussed. You do not want them to feel that they are being criticized or that they must know everything that you ask. You want to avoid putting them on the defensive by setting a conversational tone that is inviting and comforting. Then, they can really learn more about themselves.

Most beginning peer facilitators find it easy to ask questions. "You ask too many questions," said one person who was working with a peer facilitator. This person went on to say that it seemed like the facilitator was going to come up with some good solutions, based on all the questions that were being asked. After awhile the person came to see the facilitator as an interrogator, someone who was not very accepting or understanding. Consequently, you need to be somewhat cautious of only asking questions.

You can increase the use of the other high facilitative responses by simply turning questions into statements. Behind every question is usually an assumption and you can discover it by eliminating the opening word of the questions (e.g. are, do, what, why, how, and so forth) and by changing the inflection in your tone of voice. Notice how these questions were changed into facilitative statements.

Closed Question: *"Are you planning to do it?"*

Statement: *"You're planning to do it."* *(Clarifying)*

Open Question: *"How did you feel when you got an A grade that you didn't expect?"*

Statement: *"You were surprised and happy to get that A grade."* *(Feeling)*

Before we look at some more high facilitative responses, you might think of how the first three that we have already discussed can be used in various combinations. That is, you could ask an open question and then clarify the response. This could encourage someone to continue talking, giving you more opportunity to pick up on the dominant feeling or emotions that are part of the conversation.

After you ask a question, try to make a feeling-focused response next. If the feeling is not clear, then clarify. Or, after a few questions and clarifying responses, make a point to reflect the feelings that seem to be evident. About the time a person is ready to get closure on a theme or to pursue a new direction in the conversation, you may want to summarize a few key ideas or themes before asking the next open question.

Try to keep your own statements short and to the point. When you string together several of your own comments, the person will tend to hear the last thing that you said and respond to it. Thus, if you want a feeling-focused response to have impact, let it stand by itself after you make it (e.g. "You were angry"). Avoid tying a question to it (e.g. "So, you were angry and how did you handle that?"). Use pauses prudently.

Some helpers have found that using a combination of these first three facilitative responses is all that is needed in the helping process. They keep the focus on the person who is being helped. When combined with the problem-solving model (Chapter 6) the responses can be used in many different situations. When the facilitative process relies on these first three high facilitative responses, the responsibility for decision making and problem solving rests squarely on the helpee's shoulders. The helper is only assisting the person to become aware of influential factors, such as feelings and the major ideas or events.

Facilitative feedback: Complimenting and confronting

The first three high facilitative responses keep the focus on people whom you are helping—their feelings and ideas. As you listen to them talk, you will be moved to have some of your own impressions. You will find yourself reacting to things that they say or do. How and when do you share your own feelings and ideas?

We want to know what others think of us. It is human nature. We almost always prefer a compliment to a confrontation, but any form of feedback lets us know the kind of impact that we are having on others. We learn who we are by the reactions that people have to us.

Our behavior is influenced by the consequences of our actions. Sometimes the consequences are clear and at other times they are not. For instance, if you spend time around some people, you may not know how they see you unless they tell you. You may have to read between the lines and to guess as to whether they see you as a friend or not. How would they describe you to others? What do you do that gives them their impressions? What feelings do they get when they are with you? The answer to these and other questions would provide you with *feedback* about yourself and probably prove to be some valuable information. It would be especially useful if you wanted to use the information to change something about yourself.

When you receive feedback from others, you then know the kind of impact that you are having on them. You know more about the consequences of your actions with them. You can decide whether you want to continue doing similar things or to change your behaviors.

In a similar vein, many of the people with whom you will be working as a peer facilitator will want to know how you see them. They will want to know what impact they are having on you. They will want to know what you are thinking and feeling about them.

Feedback, when given in a facilitative way as a compliment or a confrontation, can provide helpful information about behavior and it can also be used to improve relationships between people. In general, facilitative feedback consists of three parts. These are:

Part 1: Be specific about the behavior. You might begin by saying, "One of the things that I've noticed about you is...." Give an example. Be specific about what the person has done. Cite a time when the person did what you are focusing on. It does not help to use general labels (e.g. You're a nice person; You are cooperative and kind; or, You are mean and insensitive). If you have a label in mind, think of the specific behaviors that led you to conclude such a label. Providing specifics by describing what you have heard and seen is essential in facilitative feedback.

Part 2: Tell how the behavior makes you feel. Now take stock of your own feelings when you are in the presence of that behavior. Sort out your feelings by searching your feeling word vocabulary list. Is it a pleasant or unpleasant feeling? You might pick one or two feelings that stand out in order to tell the person what you are experiencing when the person acts that way.

Part 3: Tell what your feelings make you want to do. After considering your feelings, how do you want to respond? You are, of course, responsible for your feelings and behaviors. To have a feeling does not necessarily mean that you have to act it out, but it can be helpful to let a person know the kind of things that you feel like doing or saying. It is important to identify specifically what the person's behavior makes you want to do. What behavior does it tend to elicit from you? For practice, see if you can identify the three parts of facilitative feedback in the following response:

"Max, one of the things I've noticed about you is that you are a very good listener. By that I mean, you look at people when they talk and you ask questions to help them think about their ideas. You did that with me, yesterday, when we were talking about my ideas for the science club. That makes me feel special and important. It makes me want to continue our friendship even more, and I wanted you to know that before we started the meeting today."

Now, try this example. Look for the three different parts.

"Andrea, I'm confused and upset. I need to talk with you and see if we can straighten some things out. You see, you said that you were going to pick me up to go shopping on Friday night, then you

said it might be Saturday morning, and now you are thinking about not going at all."

Max received a compliment in the first example. You can see that all three parts were included in the order of 1,2,3. After starting with a label, the feedback became more specific. In the case of Andrea, the three parts appeared in a different order (2,3,1) and were the basis of a confrontation. Andrea was hearing about the kind of unpleasant impact that her behavior was having on someone.

The parts of the facilitative feedback model can be interchanged. Using the examples given above, how would it sound if the parts were rearranged? Would it make a difference in how the feedback would be received? Does it affect the message to be given? Sometimes placement can create a different emphasis, but the feedback is still the same.

As you become more adept at giving compliments and confrontations through the feedback model, you will also notice that it tends to slow the communication down. It helps you to collect and organize your thoughts and feelings. It increases the probability that you will communicate them accurately and effectively. In that sense, the parts are like the elements of a well-structured paragraph or perhaps a math formula, each contributing a valuable factor in order to accomplish a goal.

The difference between compliments and confrontations is found in Part 2. If you find that someone's actions cause you to experience *pleasant* feelings (again perhaps drawing upon your feeling word

list), then you are likely to be in a position to give a *compliment*. On the other hand, if the actions produce *unpleasant* feelings within you, then your feedback is probably going to come across as a *confrontation*.

Confrontations are not judgments of people. They are not labels or put-downs. Rather, they attempt to let persons know more about what you are experiencing, based on what they have done, and what it makes you feel like doing. Confrontations, no matter how gentle, tend to make people defensive. Therefore, after confronting someone, it is essential to be ready to facilitate them in exploring the issues.

For instance, in our example, Andrea may have become defensive and tried to explain how the confusion came about. A possible next response might have been:

"I can see, Andrea, that you're frustrated. You were in a bind and were unsure what to do. What could you have done to have helped me not become so upset and confused?"

Such a response after the confrontation would have followed Andrea's lead, focusing on her feelings. An open-ended question, perhaps encouraging the two parties to explore the matter more is the last statement. The confrontation and follow-up conversation is intended to clarify the situation, provide some feedback, and to bring the two people closer together as friends. When people avoid giving feedback, for fear that it might be misunderstood or that the person probably already knows, there are missed opportunities for closer communication and the building of caring and personal relationships.

You can compliment or confront an individual. You can also compliment or confront a group of people, perhaps members of a discussion group. This can be tricky since it lumps many behaviors together, but it can also help bond a group together. For example:

"Before we get started today, I want to say something (Part 3). I've noticed that all of us are getting to the meetings on time and that everyone is participating in some way or another. For example, last week everyone in the room had at least one idea or reaction to an idea about our spring event (Part 1). As your president, I find that really encouraging and it makes me proud to work with you (Part 2)."

There are three guidelines that might be helpful when considering a confrontation. First, the unpleasant feelings that you are experiencing should be rather persistent. If you confront everyone every time that you feel uneasy, you are likely to come across as a grumpy, unhappy person. Some confrontations cannot wait. They are needed at the moment and there is no opportunity to postpone or delay. But, if you can take note of your unpleasant feelings and hold off on your reactions, preferring to facilitate the other person with other responses if you can, you may gain some more information which will be useful to you when it is time to confront. You may even find that a confrontation is not needed.

Second, you should have some "chips in the bank." That is an expression that we use to refer to the first three high facilitative responses (feeling-focused, clarifying or summarizing, and open questions). These responses help create the kind of relationship that makes the person more open and receptive to your feedback. In a manner of speaking, you are going to probably cash in a few of those chips when you confront someone. If you have a reserve which you can draw upon, then you are probably not going to threaten your relationship. If you have a friendly, caring, and open relationship, then confrontation, when timely, can be helpful to both parties and actually enhance the relationship.

Finally, you will also want to consider your choice of words. Some words and phrases may come across as too harsh or unkind. Select those words that best describe what you are experiencing but that are also sensitive to the person's situation.

You can communicate that you are irritated or frustrated, rather than angry or mad, if that is the case. You can choose to say that you feel restless and fatigued rather than bored or irritated. Certain unpleasant feelings are perceived as so intense that they might steer persons off on a different course, perhaps making them so defensive that communication is closed off. This is also true of what your feelings make you want to do. It is probably more facilitative to say that your unpleasant feelings make you want to talk with the person, or ask that person what is going on, rather than "You make me so mad that I never want to speak with you again."

You will find your own style in giving feedback. The three parts will be helpful, but you must decide on what words you will use and what your feelings make you want to do. Some people have a greater range of feelings and choice of behaviors than others. As you learn more about yourself and others, your ability to compliment and confront will improve. You will also learn that you can elicit feedback from others as well as give it yourself.

Now let us take a look at the final two high facilitative responses. They are typically used when working with groups.

Simple acknowledgment

After someone has said something, that person often looks for some kind of acknowledgment as to whether anyone heard what was said or not. In groups, members like to have their contributions acknowledged before someone else talks or the topic is changed. Otherwise, they might feel ignored and embarrassed. Consequently, simple acknowledgment has made the list of our six high facilitative responses. Here are a few examples:

"Thank you."

"All right."

"Okay."

"Thanks for sharing that."

You can be more expansive in your words, but it is usually not necessary to help avoid a "plop experience," when nobody responds and you feel rejected. You do not have to say, "That's great!" or "Wow, that was really interesting." Keeping it simple means to limit the language of the acknowledgment and to avoid excessive praise or attention.

Simple acknowledgments are a form of "putting a period down." The person to whom you are responding is given credit for a contribution, but is not encouraged to continue talking at that time. The simple acknowledgment has a way of bringing closure to a person's contribution at that moment and opens the door for others to respond. It can be a polite way of saying that you are now ready to hear from someone else.

Linking

Another facilitative response that can be helpful when leading a group discussion is linking. This is an attempt to pair or link similar events or ideas (content) that have been shared by certain group members. It can also be used to pair or link any feelings that people seem to have in common. Look at these examples:

"Allen and Jennifer, you both are trying to find a way to manage your time, so that you can get more accomplished." (Content linked).

"Allen and Jennifer, you're disappointed with how you manage your time." (Feelings linked).

Linking people through the feelings, events, or ideas that they have in common has a way of bonding a group. It helps create a sense of togetherness. Linking responses emphasize relationships and help set a tone of acceptance, understanding, and mutual respect. The responses are especially valuable when working with group members who differ in gender, age, race, or culture.

Low Facilitative Responses

You are going to say a lot of things when you are working as a peer helper. Some of the things you say will probably be more facilitative than others. As suggested above, you want to increase the use of the six high facilitative responses because they help you to be viewed as a caring, understanding, accepting, and friendly helper. They also encourage the people you are helping to do most of the work, thinking aloud about various issues and situations. When used in combinations with some general strategies that you will learn later, the six basic high facilitative responses will make your work go well. You will feel more productive and satisfied with the helping process.

There are still other things that you can say and do. Research has shown that some responses to people can be helpful, but they are much less likely to be facilitative. We call those the low facilitative responses. We hear them quite often in our daily lives. You will recognize them and may think of times when they were helpful to you. Yet, because they are used so often by so many people, they may be part of the reason why they are less facilitative. Three low facilitative responses that will receive our attention are: reassuring/supporting; analyzing/interpreting; and, advising/evaluating.

Robert D. Myrick and Betsy E. Folk

Reassuring/Supporting

There are many times when people want to encourage and be supportive, but they do not know what to say or do. They try to be reassuring, hoping that their comments will be helpful. Look at these examples:

"Hey, everything is going to turn out okay."

"It's no big deal... you'll be all right after awhile."

"You can do it."

"I know how you feel."

"I understand what you're going through."

"It's going to be okay tomorrow."

"Everyone feels that way about their parents."

"It's always dark before the sun shines."

For the lack of a better term we call these reassuring/supporting statements. The aim is usually to bolster the person's spirit—to offer some hope. However, more often than not these well-intended responses miss the mark. Instead of feeling understood and supported, a person hearing such comments often feels misunderstood, unaccepted, even rejected. These statements frequently fail to be facilitative because they ignore or dismiss the person's feelings.

Too often reassuring/supporting kinds of responses send the message that people should not feel as they do. Rather, things will be better soon, so move on and do not go through what you are experiencing now. In that sense there is some unspoken advice: "Stop feeling the way you do and keep hanging in there."

On occasion, statements such as those listed above may very well be perceived as helpful. Timely reassurance and support can be valuable. If you rush in with reassuring/supporting type responses, you are likely to discourage the person from talking, from exploring the matter in more depth. The typical reaction to such responses is to acknowledge them and then change the subject or topic.

"I was just trying to build their self-confidence," was what one beginning peer facilitator reported. He had told a group of new students that "all students feel uncomfortable when they are just starting high school." He said that he felt the same way when he was their age, too. Later, he recognized that his remarks were responsible for the group discussion bogging down. It made it more difficult for some members to share their feelings. He concluded, "If I had stayed with the high facilitative responses, the group would have felt supported anyway, since I would have showed them that I really understood and was with them." He was probably right.

Analyzing/Interpreting

Another low facilitative response is called analyzing/interpreting. It is assumed that there is a logical and reasonable explanation for everything someone does. Therefore, analyzing and interpreting one's behavior will provide more insight to a problem or situation and pave the way for decision making and change. These responses are easy to recognize since they often have or imply the word "because" in them. Look at these examples:

"You want to change classes in order to be with your closest friends."

"The reason you want to drop the math class is because you're falling behind in your work and think you can't catch up."

"You don't want to go to college because you don't have much money."

"Don't you see that gossiping about her was just another way of saying how much she had hurt your feelings when she didn't invite you to go along?"

"The only thing you think about is football because it's one place where you get a lot of attention."

The purpose of these responses is to explain the person's behavior, to hopefully provide some insight. They are telling the person what they should or ought to be thinking.

The reasons given for one's behavior may or may not be true since there are usually many factors that influence a person's actions. Even therapists and certified counselors, who have more specialized training in human behavior and helping relationships, consider this low facilitative response to be risky. It too often is confronting and comes from a superior position, which makes people defensive.

Timely interpretations, perhaps better phrased as hypotheses, might be helpful at the right moment. They provide some food for thought. Even when true or reasonably accurate, however, most people resist having their behavior analyzed and interpreted to them. Therefore, such responses are considered low facilitative and must be used sparingly.

Advising/Evaluating

This may not be surprising to you, but most people who have a problem or who are in a difficult situation do not really want advice from others. They prefer to talk with someone who will be understanding and accepting and who will help them think matters through. They want a facilitator not an advisor.

Too many times, helpers cannot wait to hear a person's story. They sometimes forget to use the high facilitative skills and, in their eagerness to help, rush in with advice. They think that they have a solution or an answer that will solve the problem. They cannot resist telling the person what they should or ought to do. For instance:

"You need to study more. Forget about that last test and just get to work on the next assignment."

"Instead of complaining to me, you should go to the principal and tell what you're so mad about."

"If you would only try a little harder, maybe get some extra coaching, you'd make the team."

"One of the best things you could do right now is to talk with the teacher and say that you are sorry for what you said in class. You need to do that first or you'll never get back in class."

"Just go ahead and ask her if she'll go out with you."

Giving advice is a popular form of conversation, but it can stifle communication. If the person agrees with the advice, then there is no need to talk any more about the subject. If the person disagrees, then an element of defensiveness, perhaps even an argument may begin.

When advice is timely, practical, and relevant, it may be helpful. It can facilitate people toward their goals. When worded in the form of a suggestion, perhaps a thoughtful question, instead of a directive, timely advice may be appropriate and well received. Some possible lead-ins, in this case, might be: "What would happen if...." "One thing you might want to consider is...." "I was wondering if you have thought of...." Such introductory phrases soften the resistance to advice and let the person see them as suggestions or things to think about.

In a similar vein, evaluation statements are not well-received, even when they are meant as praise. Evaluation remarks are judgmental, whether they are positive or negative, and most people resist being judged. Evaluations such as "that's good," or "great" might be seen as reinforcing in some instances, but they are often met with some suspicion. Does it mean that in order to continue to be seen in a favorable light, that the person must continue doing what was praised? Does it also mean that if you are the kind of person who will judge one as doing positive things, will you also be one who will criticize or apply negative labels?

Again, evaluations may be appropriate on some occasions, especially when timely and when you have already built a helping relationship. Early praise or criticism, although meant well, makes most people stop talking about themselves for fear of being rejected, labeled, or judged unfairly at a later date.

In one case, a close friend told a depressed teenage girl: "You have so many good things going for you. You're pretty and smart, you get top grades and everyone likes you. You are too neat a person to do something so foolish as to kill yourself. You need to think positively about yourself." That night the girl attempted suicide by taking an overdose of medicine. Fortunately, she lived. But, all the reassurances, praise, and advice seemed to make little difference in how she was thinking about herself, the problems in her life, or her actions.

Summary

There are, no doubt, other ways of talking about high and low facilitative responses. Perhaps there are some other ways of categorizing them which may make sense to you. You may want to add other possible responses to your list of helpful things that you might do, or to make a list of responses you hope to avoid. The only way to know if a response is really facilitative is to watch for the impact that it has on others.

The low facilitative responses are questionable and must be used with caution. Ironically, these responses are so popular in everyday life that the person you are helping is likely to have heard them before. What you can do as a helper is to offer more high facilitative responses, which give others more opportunity to think about themselves.

You will have to study and practice the high facilitative responses. You will then be able to put them in problem solving combinations or make them a part of some helping activities. You will have to discipline yourself so that you will not drift into old habits which are not facilitative. As you increase the use of high facilitative responses in your work, you will find that you are a better listener and helper.

Robert D. Myrick and Betsy E. Folk

Activity 5.1
What Can Be Said?

Purpose:

To learn and practice using facilitative responses.

Materials:

Three scenarios listed below. Paper/pencil

Procedures:

1. Look at the following situations. Write a response which illustrates: a) feeling-focused, b) clarifying or summarizing, or c) a question.

   A. **Situation One:** *"I'm not sure if I should go to the concert. It's going to start very late and some of my friends have said there will be a lot of drinking."*

   B. **Situation Two:** *"That test was unfair. He* (the teacher) *tried to trick us. Nothing from the review sheet was on the test. It was a waste of time to study it."*

   C. **Situation Three:** *"I know I shouldn't have, but I did! I can't believe it. We were at the mall and someone dared me to steal some earrings which were on the counter. I thought to myself, 'Oh, why not?' and so I did. Now, I don't know what to do."*

2. Now, write one low facilitative response to each situation.

3. Underline the response that a peer helper, such as yourself, would most likely give.

4. After you have written your responses, join a group of about four students and take turns reading some of your statements to each of the situations.

Key Questions:

How were your responses similar or different from what others shared? How are written responses the same or different from what might actually be said?

Activity 5.2
The Feedback Chair

Purpose:

To learn and practice facilitative feedback responses.

Materials:

An empty chair

Procedures:

1. Join a group of about five or six persons and sit in a circle. An empty chair—the feedback chair—is placed in the middle of the circle.

2. Think of someone you like. As you think of the person, what is it that person does which affects you so positively? What kind of pleasant feelings do you get? And, when you have that feeling(s), what do you want to say or do?

3. Now imagine that the person is sitting in the empty chair. Using the three parts of the feedback model, practice giving the person a compliment.

4. Others in the group can help coach you through the steps and comment after you have finished if they have heard all three parts of the model.

5. After everyone has had a turn giving a compliment to the feedback chair, think of someone whom you would like to confront. What unpleasant feeling do you have when the person does a certain thing. Now, give that person some feedback, speaking to the empty chair again.

6. Discuss the experience with the group after everyone has had a turn talking to the feedback chair.

Key Questions:

Was it easier to compliment or confront someone? Which of the three parts of the feedback model were most difficult to put into your statement? Is it possible that you could really give the persons you were thinking about such feedback? What would get in the way of your doing so?

Decision Making and Problem Solving

Marsha had saved her money to buy clothes for school. She was unsure what to buy. She wanted some mix and match outfits so she could get the most use out of her purchases, but there was one favorite dress which had caught her eye. It cost more than she was planning to spend on a single dress, but it was so appealing.

Everyday you make choices about the things to do. Sometimes your decisions are quick or spontaneous. At other times, decisions require more careful thought. Some of your casual choices are about familiar matters and are easy. On other occasions, you may find yourself in situations where you have to take more time to think matters through before you can decide.

How long does it take you, for example, to decide what to order from a lunch menu? If you are eating at school, your choices may be limited and decision making is not very difficult. Or, depending on the day of the week, you might already have an idea of what will be offered and what you almost always tend to select.

Suppose you want to go to a movie. You count your money and the amount may help you decide quickly whether or not to buy a ticket. Or, maybe your friends have asked you to go with them to a movie you have already seen. Now, you have a another problem. Even though you have the money, you have to decide if the movie is worth seeing again. Other factors may enter into your decision, such as the importance of joining your friends or how else you might spend your money.

How long does it take you to make these kinds of decisions?

- To save your money or to buy a new cassette tape
- Choosing which clothes to wear to school
- Picking a time to do homework
- Saying "no" when offered an alcoholic drink
- To take a shower in the morning or at night
- Asking someone to go out with you
- Getting a job after graduation from high school or going on to college
- To get married within the next year

Some decisions are easier than others. They appear to be less involved. Considering the long range consequences, some decisions are minor while others have a way of influencing your life and, subsequently, your future choices and decisions.

Critical Issues in Decision Making and Problem Solving

Over the years many experts have studied how people make decisions and solve problems. Some scholars have outlined detailed procedures and discussed the many factors which enter into the process. The following set of questions has emerged from research and directs our attention to the critical issues.

Robert D. Myrick and Betsy E. Folk

What is the problem?

A problem is a question calling for a solution. It is a situation that is perplexing or troublesome. There is usually a degree of confusion and uncertainty while it is being resolved. You may need to ask yourself, "What is it that I am facing?" Or, "What is the real issue here?"

The first step in decision making is identifying the problem. What exactly is it that you want to make a decision about?

Kevin was having trouble in school. He had low grades and almost daily conflicts with teachers. He was thinking of dropping out of school to get a job, even though he was only sixteen. He was tired "of being hassled" and self-conscious of having so few clothes and so little spending money. What was Kevin's problem?

One of his friends thought that Kevin's problem was his frequent absence from school and that he seldom turned in his class assignments. The assistant principal said Kevin's problem was his negative attitude about school and not getting along with teachers. The school counselor thought the problem was related to an unkind and unsupportive stepfather who made it difficult for Kevin to like home or school. To Kevin, the problem was simple: How can I get a job and earn some money?

Perhaps all of the observations that people made about Kevin played a part in his difficult situation. There seemed to be many related problems. There were also a lot of choices and decisions, each with consequences. If Kevin resolved one problem, would it in turn help resolve

another? For instance, if Kevin were to decide to attend class and study more, would that help rid him of the problems he is having with teachers and help him like school more? Or, if he decided to get a part-time job after school, would that help him feel better about himself?

What is the real problem? If the problem is complex, then which parts of it should receive attention first? What decisions need to be made?

Some people find it helpful to work with paper and pencil, listing their problems in order to see which ones are related. It is a visual aide to identify those factors that need the most attention or highest priority. With a list in hand, it may be easier to determine which immediate decisions must be made and which ones can be resolved the fastest and easiest. In addition, studying the written problems, including the terms and words used to pose the questions, may provide some clues as to the real issues and possible solutions.

Look at Kevin's list:

School is boring.

I hate school.

I am too far behind in my classes.

I need money.

I need a job.

I wish my mother weren't such a nag.

My stepfather is a bum.

Teachers don't care if I pass or fail.

Mr. Stevens (the assistant principal) is a $#%!!.

Where should Kevin start? What is his problem? Remember, he sees his problem as trying to decide whether to stay in school or dropout and get a job.

All of us are problem solvers in one way or another. It is our daily job. Many of the problems facing us are resolved by our daily routines, habits, general skills, and without too much thought. Some "big" problems may be the result of the build up of many "smaller" problems. There is an accumulation of indecision and, subsequently, frustration and stress.

In addition to writing problems down, it can also be helpful to talk them out. You may have a friend who listens to your problems, helping you sort out the issues or primary decisions which have to be made. Or, perhaps you have an adult advisor, counselor, or parent who will hear you out. Peer facilitators, of course, are trained listeners. They help people think about their problems and give them the luxury of exploring their ideas and feelings in a trusting atmosphere.

What are the choices?

Once the problem or problems have been identified, then it is time to consider the choices. What options do you have?

What are Kevin's alternatives to dropping out of school? To being bored in class? To hating school? Working with a peer helper, he considered, among other things: full-time, part-time, and not having any job. They also talked about asking for assistance from "Catch Up Helpers," a peer tutoring project, meeting with teachers, or setting aside more time for study on his own. They further explored the options of staying at home, finding a place of his own, or living with his widowed aunt.

Linda and Gary were at a party when they noticed that a few people were smoking marijuana. "Hey, you wanna hit?" They both responded "no" and moved on to another room. Even though the music was great and the dancing was fun, they both agreed to leave. "We just don't want to be around people who do drugs," they later told some friends who asked about them. "We really didn't want to leave, but just being there is the same as saying it's okay to smoke. We didn't want to give that message."

Robert D. Myrick and Betsy E. Folk

What are the consequences?

The third step usually involves thinking about the consequences of the options or choices. What would happen if you made certain choices? What might result if a certain decision was made? Would one choice be better than the other in terms of time, money, energy, or skill needed? How would the choices affect other parts of my life, such as personal relationships or future goals and choices?

If Kevin quit school at an early age, he was going to limit his job opportunities and depend, for the most part, on training which he might receive on a job. He was going to rid himself of unpleasant feelings related to school, but he was also limited to the kind of job he might obtain. He would end conflicts with his teachers, but would similar expectations (getting to work on time, being reliable, following directions and following through on assignments) come from his employer? Would there be similar conflicts?

Considering the possible consequences and making the best decision might not be possible without additional information. You may ask, "What are the facts?" Or, "What data do I need to have in order to make the best decision?"

In the process of collecting more information, you may also discover that there are more alternatives than you first thought. For example, when Kevin started to look for a job, he learned that a vocational education course was being offered at a nearby technical school. He could get

a part-time job and go to school at the same time. He also learned that the school would not accept him unless he was in good standing with his regular school, including a good attendance record. He began considering the consequences of some of his choices.

What is the decision?

After considering the possible results of the alternatives, you try to choose the best one. In addition to thinking about positive and negative consequences, advantages and disadvantages, and possible rewards or personal satisfaction, you eventually tend to make a decision based on what you think is most important to you.

You may have to do some more searching, perhaps in terms of your personal values. What you believe to be true or what you think is worthwhile tends to shape your attitudes and the way you see things. These perceptions, in turn, influence your choices.

You may prize honesty, knowledge, athletic skill, social prestige, friendship, physical well-being, or spiritual growth. Some of these may be more personally meaningful and valuable to you than others. Not everyone has the same values and goals. Not everyone is looking for the same kind of rewards or fulfillment.

Have you ever thought about what you value most? Which of the following items do you value most?

Being alone vs. Being with others

Music vs.
Athletics

Listening to a speaker vs.
Reading a newspaper

Saving money vs.
Spending for fun

Recognition from others vs.
Self-satisfaction

Having a close family vs.
Having close friends

Buying a car vs.
Buying the latest clothes

Going to the movies vs.
Going to a dance

Watching TV vs.
Reading a book

Are your values, or choices, the same as your parents? How are they the same or different from your closest friend? From someone who sits next to you in your third period class? How much do you know about yourself and the things which influence you to make decisions?

Lawrence Kohlberg, who was a Harvard psychologist, studied stages of moral development. He suggested that when we are small children, we first learn to think and act out of fear and a desire for reward and favors. Then, as we grow older and become more socialized, we act according to expectations that authorities (e.g. parents, teachers, police) have for us. Finally, as we become more mature and educated, we think, make decisions, and act on the basis of moral principals that are genuinely accepted.

Responsible, mature people seek an awareness of the factors which shape their decisions and development. They try to know more about habits, religious training, family attitudes, local traditions, public media, and other sources which influence morals, personalities, and decision making.

Regardless of your decisions, you must be responsible for your choices. If you spontaneously make a choice without regard to consequences and, subsequently, are unhappy, you have to assume responsibility for the results and unhappiness. And, you must also assume responsibility for making some new decisions which will make things better.

Kevin was convinced that dropping out of school was the best way to solve a lot of problems. He would experience relief from the pressures of school work and teachers. However, it also meant that he could not come on campus to see his friends. While he could get some part-time work, he was too young and his skills were too limited to get the kind of job he wanted most.

Roxanne had to have her own car. She liked the idea of "sportin' around in my own car" and knew it would make her more popular with her friends. So, she spent her summer savings and found an after school job to help pay for a used car. However, she forgot about insurance costs.

Then, one day the muffler fell off and had to be replaced. Shortly thereafter, the battery went dead and she learned that she needed two new tires. "I had no idea that it was going to cost me so much extra money. I'm having trouble just making the payment. And, gas money has taken away most of my spending money. I haven't bought any new clothes in months. I have a car, but sometimes it has to just sit in the driveway. I'm thinking of selling it."

Roxanne made a decision which appealed to her. She valued her car, but then realized that one decision had an impact on many other parts of her life. For her, the decision was reversible, but not until she had given up time, money, and other pleasurable things for awhile.

Amber decided that she wanted to be a part of "Drug-Free 2000" and she was adamant about not smoking or being around those who smoked. She learned some refusal skills which were socially acceptable to others and became an active member of the "Just Say No Club." Amber made a decision and acted on it.

What should be done now?

Almost all decisions involve an action—some kind of behavior. Even if the decision is to change our attitude, that attitude is going to be reflected in the things we do. Making a decision and following through with some responsible action may take courage and strength, especially if it involves a challenge.

Rebecca was not getting the kind of grades she hoped for. She studied hard, but performed poorly on tests. On the final exam for the six weeks grading period, she thought of sneaking a peek at some notes. Using notes was not allowed, although a few students did. It was wrong, but the pressure to get a good grade weighed heavily.

Suddenly, Rebecca reached down and slid out her crib notes. She was so nervous that she could not read her own hand writing at first. She quickly put the notes down, having barely read the names and dates she had listed in case her memory failed her. A second peek gave her the answers she was seeking.

When Rebecca received her grade, she was initially pleased. But a classmate said rudely, "Sure, it was an easy test for those who cheated!" The words cut deep and there was no way to defend her actions. She had made a poor decision, was caught in the act, and now had to live with the consequences, being called a cheater. Her grade had no meaning anymore, for it was obtained dishonestly.

"A person who will cheat in one situation will probably cheat in another," said another student. Rebecca's guilt was heavy and she considered herself a fraud. She decided, on her own, to talk with the teacher and admit to having made a poor decision. She vowed at that moment to study harder and in the future to resist the urge to be so deceptive.

Rebecca made a lot of decisions, some snowballing into others. It took courage and determination to talk with her teacher about the matter. It was not an easy course of action, but it did set things straight and give back her personal pride.

What was the result?

Evaluating the outcomes of your decisions and actions is the last step of any problem solving process. Sometimes it is obvious that you are satisfied with the results of what you have decided to do and your actions. If you are not sure, there are ways to "get a reading" on where you were when you started and where you are now. Recording some baseline data can be helpful when you try to assess the gains you have made.

Kevin decided to improve his attendance at school. He looked at his tardiness and absentee record for the preceding six weeks. He decided to change his teachers' perceptions of him. He decided that he would be on time to class and, even though he was not always prepared, he would at least attend all of his classes.

In comparison to the preceding grading period, Kevin's attendance record improved. He attended class 40% more of the time. He also turned in more assignments. "Well, since I was there I thought I might as well keep myself busy by finishing a few of the worksheets here and there...." Going to class was still dull for Kevin, but his grades improved a little and his teachers noticed the positive change. One decision had led to another and a string of behaviors were tied together which helped Kevin do better in his school work.

Peer Facilitators and Problem Solving

Helping others to think about how to solve problems is a complex task. First, you will want to know more about yourself and how you tend to make your own decisions. What are your goals and what are your hopes for the future?

If you are to help others, you must guard against pushing your own values and goals upon others. The decision you might make in their situations may not be the best one for them. Rather than judge or advise, you can be of most assistance by encouraging them to explore ideas and discover solutions for themselves. There may be times when you think the answer to a problem is obvious and you may even wonder why the person keeps missing it. On the other hand, the person could be thinking, "Why is this helper trying so hard to convince me what to do? It's my problem and my life."

Part of your training is learning restraint. Learn to focus your attention on others. Listen carefully to what is being said so that you can clarify and summarize key points that have been made. Part of your job is to help others focus their thinking so that they can fully grasp their situations, the problems which face them, the decisions they are trying to make, and the responsibility that they have for the actions they take as individuals.

Summary

As a peer facilitator, you will be a problem solver. However, this does not mean you will provide answers, give advice, or take responsibility for someone else's problem. You will not make decisions or take action for them. Rather, as a peer helper, you will guide them through the decision-making process. By using the facilitative skills and models presented in this book, they will feel supported and empowered.

Here are four open ended questions which make up a four-step problem solving model. You can use these questions as a guide when working with someone who is trying to make a decision.

Step One: *What is the problem or situation?*

Step Two: *What have you done?*

Step Three: What else could you do?

Step Four: *What is your next step?*

These four questions clarify the issues, especially when you follow with other facilitative responses. These questions focus the responsibility on the person being helped.

Most people can benefit from thinking about what they have already done to solve their problems. Step Two encourages them to reflect on what has been accomplished. In addition, it may emphasize that very little or nothing has actually been tried to this point. Many people are resourceful and have attempted several things, but have not been able to resolve the problem.

If you have any suggestions, they might be offered in Step Three, but only after the person has run out of ideas. You might also ask in Step Three about the possible consequences of each option that is presented. "How do you think it might turn out, if you did that?" Or, "If you did that, what do you think might happen?"

As part of Step Four, you may assist the person to sort out some different actions, including those which upon more thought are practical and workable. It can also be helpful to think of a time when a plan of action could be started.

Listen for opportunities to use the high facilitative responses when the person with whom you are working responds to a question. Are you hearing pleasant or unpleasant feelings? How would you summarize what has been said? What are the key ideas so far?

Robert D. Myrick and Betsy E. Folk

Activity 6.1
The Earthquake

Purpose:

To practice setting priorities and making decisions.

Materials:

Paper and pencil

Procedures:

1. Imagine that you have been forewarned of an earthquake that is about to destroy your house and city. Everyone is moving to safer ground and there is no assurance that you will be able to return again. The city is likely to cave in and be lost forever. You have only enough time to run home and save ten things that are important to you, besides family members.

2. Make a list of the ten things you would most want to save.

3. After you make the list, you then receive an announcement that you may Take only five things from your list because both time and transportation are limited. Rank order your top five choices.

4. After all class members have individually completed and ranked their lists, form groups of about five or six members each. Discuss your choices and your reasons for them.

Key Questions:

How did this activity help you learn about what you value? What did you experience when you learned that you could take only five items from your list? What ideas came to mind as you made your list and set your priorities? How are your choices different from those of other group members? How are they the same?

Activity 6.2
The Problem Solving Model

Purpose:

To practice the four-step problem solving model.

Materials:

Paper and pencil

Procedures:

1. Get into a group of three (triad). Number off, 1, 2, and 3.

2. Number 1 is the facilitator and will use the four-step problem solving model with Number 2, who will talk about a problem or a decision that he or she is trying to make. Number 3 will be an observer, recording the kinds of responses that the facilitator uses in addition to the four basic questions: 1) What is the problem or situation? 2) What have you tried? 3) What else could you do? 4) What is your next step?

3. If you are short of time, the facilitator will make only three or four high facilitative responses (e.g. feeling-focused, clarifying or summarizing, or how and what questions) during each step. This is a practice session and the problem need not be explored in depth.

4. After about six minutes, the observer takes about one or two minutes to share observations and the data that were recorded.

5. After the first round, the roles are rotated and there is then a new facilitator, observer, and talker.

6. A third round is completed in order to give everyone in the triad an opportunity to play each part.

7. Now, talk about your experiences.

Key Questions:

How did the problem solving model work in each situation? What did you experience as the facilitator? The talker? What observations were made by the observers? Can you identify the high and low facilitative responses that were used with the four key questions? Was this activity helpful to you?

Robert D. Myrick and Betsy E. Folk

Chapter 7

It is Time to Help Others

You have been studying ways to be a peer facilitator. Now, it is time to put your skills to work. Helping others to realize more of their potential and to enjoy life can be a special experience for them and for you.

The basic communication skills that you have been learning and practicing are only part of the helping process. The models and strategies you have been studying are no more than guidelines. They suggest how you might approach matters systematically and they increase the chances of your being successful. But, by themselves they lack the special personal ingredient which you can provide.

You can do things which help others see you as caring, interested, respectful, understanding, and trustworthy. If others see you this way, then they are more likely to share their thoughts and feelings with you. There is a better chance that they will let you help them look closer at some of the important events in their lives.

The six high facilitative responses can make your work easier. Those responses are: feeling-focused; clarifying or summarizing; open questions, especially what and how questions, feedback (complimenting and confronting), simple acknowledgments and pairing in groups. Again, none of these by themselves are sufficient to make much of a difference. Yet, when used frequently and in various combinations, they help form powerful working relationships. They contribute to your image as a helper. At the same time, the responses focus attention on the persons you are helping. You are giving them the luxury of time to think about themselves and their decisions.

You will also recall that sometimes these high facilitative responses can be used within a "game plan." One useful model, for example, is the four-step problem solving model (What's the problem or situation? What have you tried? What else can you do? What's your next step?").

No doubt the trainer or coordinator of your program will help you think of other things that you can do. You can apply them in the roles of counselor/teacher assistant, tutor, special friend, or small group leader. These roles form the basis around which to design projects in and out of your school.

The term peer facilitator has been used throughout this book. You and your friends may choose to refer to yourself in some other way. Regardless of what name you prefer to be called, it is the helping process that is important.

The Helping Process

No matter whether you are working with an individual or several people in a group, your first task is to be attentive to what is being said and done. Listening and observing is central to whatever else you might do.

What is your job?

Not everyone will be sure of what to say to you. Some will wonder why they have been picked to meet with you and what they are suppose to do when they are with you. There is usually an initial period of uneasiness when you first get started, as you and whomever you are working with are not quite sure what is going to happen. This can be an exciting time for both of you, especially if you are honest and candid. There is no need to try to be something you are not. Perhaps one of the first things you will want to do is to explain your "job" or assignment to them.

You might begin by introducing yourself as a peer facilitator, or by the name used by your peer helper class or group. You could say something like this:

"My name is _____. I'm a peer facilitator and I work with Mr./Mrs. _____. There are several of us who have been studying and working together. Our job is to help people talk and think about things. Sometimes we just explore different ideas and sometimes we look at decisions people are trying to make. Sometimes we talk about fun and silly things and at other times we talk about special interests, concerns, or problems. A lot of what you and I do will

depend on how well we get to know and trust each other. I thought we might begin today by...."

A get acquainted activity might follow. It could involve an exchange of general information where you are getting to know more about each other. It does not have to be a serious discussion. To the contrary, many effective helpers begin on a light note, talking about topics which are of general interest to one another.

Through these early exchanges, first impressions are formed. Therefore, regardless of the topic or the role you are playing, you will want to increase the frequency of the high facilitative responses. It is through these first exchanges and responses that you create the image of being a patient, understanding, and sensitive listener. Your actions will speak for themselves, perhaps more than any prepared statement you might read or say about your role.

What are the helper roles?

We have already mentioned the basic four helper roles: teacher/counselor assistant; tutor; special friend; and small group leader. You will work in projects, designed by both you and others, in which you can work in one or more of these roles.

As an assistant to teachers or counselors, you might take part in your school's registration procedures, perhaps passing out and helping explain the school handbook. Or, you might assist a counselor to talk with a group of students about career information.

Tutoring can spotlight academic or social skills. One peer facilitator coached a student in a few fundamental math skills. The student learned and practiced working with word problems which featured the use of fractions. Another peer helper tutored a young student in how to run an obstacle course and, subsequently, to improve her grade in a physical education class.

As special friends, peer facilitators have worked as big brothers and sisters to elementary students. In one case, a high school boy befriended a depressed fourth grade boy whose father was dying of cancer. Another high school peer helper was assigned to the in-school suspension room and talked with students who were having problems adjusting to school.

By leading a small group discussion for perhaps four or five sessions, peer facilitators can be productive in the prevention of either academic or social problems. Two peer leaders co-led a middle school drug abuse prevention unit. They used activities to increase student awareness of refusal skills.

Problem-centered or prevention?

Some projects and helper roles will be problem-centered. They will be directed to specific needs and interests, many of which have resulted from conflicts and difficult times that have burdened students. These problems can be identified through needs assessments, referrals from teachers and counselors, and self-referrals from students who know about the peer helper program.

Other projects will give attention to prevention. They may be developmental in nature. That is, they tend to focus on topics related to a particular stage of development. At various ages in life there are certain issues which demand more attention than others. In addition, when individuals learn skills in advance of a problem, then they have a better chance of resolving the problem successfully. They are better equipped to prevent a problem from occurring or escalating.

The prevention of alcohol and drug abuse is an example of a topic which has become the battle cry of many young people who aspire to have a drug-free society by the year 2000. Rather than wait until people have a problem with drugs, these students want to present useful information, increase awareness, and provide opportunities to discuss the issues, the alternatives, and goals.

Information and exploration of the prevention education topics can take place individually or in small groups as early as kindergarten and be led by peer facilitators.

The second half of this book addresses prevention education. It reviews the extent of some problems which face our society and emphasizes how peer facilitators can make a positive difference. Particular attention is given to the prevention of academic failure, suicide and depression, eating disorders, family distress, alcohol and drug abuse, bodily assault, career indecision, community unrest, and sex-related problems.

Stages of the Helping Process

With the help of your trainer and supervisor, you will study the helping process and its stages. For the most part, there is a general flow of events that take place in a rather systematic fashion. Being aware of basic stages will give you a sense of direction and suggest how you might best use your time, skills, and energy. Let us take a closer look at six helping stages.

Getting acquainted and showing that you care

Your first task is to become better acquainted with whomever you are working. Using your skills, you will try to establish a helping relationship where the facilitative conditions are evident: caring, understanding, acceptance, respect, friendliness, and trust.

Some of the best helpers know how to reach out and show that they care about others. Too many times, people who need help are shy, embarrassed, uncertain, or defensive. Your effectiveness may depend on your willingness to initiate a working relationship.

Identifying a topic, situation, or problem

After some time in which you become acquainted and talk about general interests, you begin to focus your work. You can contract for a few meetings or sessions regarding a particular topic, situation, or problem. This can lead to a more efficient

Robert D. Myrick and Betsy E. Folk

use of time, no matter whether a certain problem is identified or a general area of interest is explored. Prevention education, for example, centers activities and discussion on specific goals and objectives related to social issues.

Sometimes the problem is not always easy to identify. You may need to let a person ramble, think aloud, and move from one topic to another, as that person tries to capture the most important issue. In some cases, you might accept the presenting problem as a starting point, perhaps redefining the problem later.

In one case, a high school girl complained to her peer facilitator that the school administration treated her unfairly and was out to get her. She described her problem as being picked on by others. After listening for awhile, the peer facilitator was able to help the girl become more aware of her own behavior and how the consequences of some of her actions caused her to be seen by teachers as uncooperative and rowdy. The problem then became: How can I change my image with others?

Exploring and discovering

Increased awareness of self and others comes through free and open discussions where ideas, feelings, and behaviors are examined. When you use your skills to help people to explore issues, an increased awareness usually follows. There is more insight. They discover more about themselves The discovery process is almost always a self-search where personal meanings and goals are found.

Some people think that it would be much easier if there were someone to advise them or to tell them what to do. Others think that it would be wonderful if there were simple solutions which would be certain to assure them success. In reality, there are no easy answers and only through exploration and discovery do any of us ever arrive at responsible decisions and actions.

Decision making and taking responsible action

There is a luxury in having an opportunity to explore a topic in detail or to work through a problem with someone who is attempting to listen and facilitate our thinking. While one can never be sure of how a decision might turn out or be certain of what steps to take, it can be helpful to set goals, identify objectives, consider alternatives, set priorities, and, finally, to identify an action plan.

As a peer facilitator, one of your tasks is to help those with whom you work to make decisions and take actions which are socially responsible, as well as beneficial to their well-being. You will not, for instance, assist someone to plan out a criminal action or encourage someone to physically or psychologically hurt others. Looking for some next steps which move a person toward a healthy and productive goal is a part of the helping process.

Who is ultimately responsible for resolving a problem? You cannot assume more responsibility than the limits of your role. If you should find yourself wondering about how much responsibility you should take, what you should do, or if you are helping a person, then consult with your trainer or supervisor. If you are worried that a person with whom you are working may act in an irresponsible way, then confront the person and talk with your trainer or supervisor about the matter. One part of being an effective helper is knowing when to ask for help and when to refer to others.

Closing

Eventually the working sessions will come to an end. Although you may like the idea of maintaining a life-long friendship, many times peer facilitators are limited in how frequently and how long they meet with their assigned "buddies" or special friends.

Being a peer facilitator does not mean that you must become a best friend of those with whom you work. The nature of the helping relationship brings people closer together and friendly bonds result. Close relationships are formed by members who are on an athletic team, for example, and these same relationships are often limited by time, place, and personal interest. Eventually, the team no longer plays together and members go their separate ways, with some remaining friends for many years. You will want to spend some time thinking about how you will end a helping relationship.

Anthony, a high school peer helper, worked with Jerome, a third grade boy, at an elementary school. They became "buddies" and Jerome looked admiringly at Anthony, his special friend. They talked about all kinds of things, sometimes while playing together on the basketball court. They explored how attitude affects team and school performance. It was not easy for either of them to say good-bye at the end of the semester, but they did. Anthony announced that they would be meeting three more times and the two talked about how they would use their time. The last meeting was a celebration of sorts, as they ate pudding-pops together on the playground. The end was not a surprise, only a fact of life.

Sometimes life long friendships have developed from what first started as a peer helper assignment. As two people become better acquainted and share personal interests, it may be a choice to continue meeting and to do things together socially.

Evaluating and following-up

Finally, it is time to evaluate the progress that has been made. You can evaluate the process, what took place during your meetings, as well as the outcomes. You can ask the people with whom you worked how they felt about your meetings and what they learned about themselves or others. You can, perhaps with the help of baseline data, think about where you were when you started the helping process, and where you are now.

Eddie hated school and seldom started his homework, which meant that he rarely turned in any assignments to his teachers. When he was assigned to a peer facilitator, note was taken as to how many class assignments were started on the day they were given, how many were completed, and how many were given to the teachers. Six weeks later, another review of these learning behaviors were examined. Eddie had made progress in all three areas.

Follow-up may come at a later date. It might be a brief meeting in which the peer helper inquires as to "How has it been going?" "What has happened since we last met?" "What are your plans now?" These cordial get-togethers can also be used to provide additional information for evaluation. Many times they are simply another expression of "I care about you and wish you the best."

Your trainer or supervisor may provide you with additional ideas about the helping stages. Sometimes other words are used to describe the stages or the process, but they are generally the same everywhere.

Confidentiality and Trust

Talking on the telephone is a favorite pastime of many teenagers. Perhaps it is something you like to do with your friends. There is a social network. It is fun to talk, to share ideas, to talk about events at school and even about other people, especially those of the opposite sex. Some parents have complained that teenagers spend too much time "gossiping" on the telephone.

Peer facilitator work is not gossip. Encouraging others to talk about their ideas and to explore some questions that are on their minds is a caring and thoughtful approach to being a friend. We know that peers usually want someone their own age to listen to them. Some topics are more complex and serious than others. The conversations may be about parents, teachers, boy and girl relationships, problems in school, educational plans, jobs, or special events around school.

Trustworthiness is always an issue, even in public or private conversations with your closest friends. What you say to a friend should not be used to hurt you. It should not be told to others without your permission. In this sense peer facilitators work along the same lines, being trained to be particularly aware of the value of privacy and trust.

The person may expect you to be a confidante and someone who can be trusted with personal information. To "leak" the problem or information to others may be a serious breach of trust. Interestingly, in many cases people in serious trouble may want you to find someone who can help them. They know you are not an expert, but you are among the "first" helpers. They trust you enough to start thinking aloud about their problems, hoping that in talking with you a practical solution will emerge. Sometimes that solution is getting help from a professional helper, such as a counselor, teacher, or other competent adult.

Making Referrals

There may be times when you learn that someone has a serious problem, one beyond your own limited skills, and needs attention from an adult. What can you do? First, helping the person to talk about the situation may help that person to realize that it is a serious situation which needs special attention from a professional helper. As the problem unfolds, and as you gain the person's trust, you can make a timely suggestion that the person talk with someone you know. You can even offer to go along, make introductions, and be there for support if needed. You might say something like this:

"I appreciate your confidence in me. I know it wasn't easy to talk about your situation, but you have. And, I agree that it's something you need to continue thinking about. You have some important decisions to make. I am concerned and I care about you. And, that makes me want to suggest that you talk with ___ (helper) _____ about your situation. Do you know ___(helper) _____? If you would like, we can go together and I'll introduce you. I will even stay with you while you are there, if you'd like. The most important thing is to talk with ____ (helper) _____ because I think this person can help."

Some referrals are more urgent than others. If you think that the person you are working with needs immediate assistance from an adult, then say so. Walk with that person to the counseling center or to whomever you think might be of most help.

If the person resists, then you will have to make a personal judgment. If the person's life or someone else's life is threatened or endangered, then tell the person you have no choice but to talk with the peer trainer or coordinator who is supervising you. You would prefer that the person take responsibility and seek additional help. But, if not, then speak up. In this case, you have the person's best interests at heart. You are considering the individual's welfare and realize that the pain, frustration, or depression can be paralyzing. It can keep someone who needs professional assistance from asking for it.

As a peer facilitator, you respect the information given to you. You want to keep matters private, realizing that they have trusted you to keep matters in confidence. And, you will respect their wishes as best you can. But, when in doubt, remember that you are not a counselor or therapist. You do not have any legal authority. You are a caring person and friend who is doing the best you can to help.

One parent complained, "My daughter never talks to me any more. She spends all of her time talking on the telephone to her friends." In this case, the parent may feel left out, perhaps even worried that her daughter is confiding her concerns and feelings in others. In some cases, telephone friends may not know how to be very facilitative. As a peer facilitator, you work systematically and are aware of your responsibilities as a helper. Parents need to think of peer facilitators as allies.

You are not expected to know all the answers. You may not know more about a particular issue than the person you are trying to help. However, your support in thinking about matters is what matters the most. Most people can solve their own problems when they have time and the resources. When in doubt, make a referral. How to make a referral and to whom is a topic that you will want to discuss with your trainer.

Some Dos and Don'ts

Peer facilitators who have been trained before you have made up a list of hints which may be of interest you. Here is what they emphasized:

Look and listen.

Sometimes the person cannot say very much. You have to use your eyes to look for feelings as well as your ears to listen for them. Be a careful listener. Listen more than you talk. Avoid interrupting, unless the persons you are helping are just rambling and need to stop and put some focus to their ideas. If you interrupt, summarize and make your point a brief one. Remember, your most important role may be that of being a listener.

Be sensitive and sensing.

As a person is talking, are you hearing pleasant, unpleasant, or both kinds of feelings? Keep a feelings word list handy for quick reference, or make one together with your group or individual. Refer to it. Being sensitive also means being aware of how difficult it is for some people to share their feelings and ideas, especially about some topics.

Take time to use facilitative responses.

If you take time to collect your thoughts, it will slow you down. Most beginning peer facilitators tend to talk too fast, rushing ahead in a flurry of words. Sometimes the words are very helpful. Slowing down gives you a chance to make high facilitative responses and creates the impression that you want to be a good listener.

Keep your responses brief.

Too many times, well-intended helpers become wordy. They start talking about themselves. They forget who the focus should be on. Keeping your responses short and to the point will keep the spotlight on the other person. It also helps you make more appropriate remarks.

Gear to the person's level.

If you are going to work with elementary school students, for example, you will want to slow down and think about their vocabulary. You will want to share ideas and stories that are appropriate for their age level.

Do not take on the problem.

It is not your problem. You can be of help, but you do not own the problem. Some peer helpers have worried and felt defeated when the person with whom they were working did not do what they would have done. Some helpers become impatient and fail to see how little changes can be a positive sign.

Focus on responsible action.

You can be of assistance by just helping people to think about their ideas. Sometimes venting feelings and talking about a situation can produce some ideas that are helpful. However, you will also want to check for the responsible action the person is going to take. It might be useful to set some goals or identify objectives. It is particularly useful to think of what might be done in the near future to make positive things happen. What will happen now? What might be done? What are the consequences? What are the alternatives? What seems to be the best next step? What will you do now with your skills? How can you help others? How can you play a part in preventive education?

Robert D. Myrick and Betsy E. Folk

Activity 7.1
Assessing the Territory

Purpose:

To develop a survey form of specific concerns, needs, and problems that are present in a school.

Materials:

Paper and pencil

Procedures:

1. The class will be divided into three or four equal groups. Each group will brainstorm a list of specific concerns, needs, and problems facing students at the school where they plan to work as peer facilitators.

2. After about eight to ten minutes, groups in turn then share with the rest of the class their items. A combined list and tally for the entire class might be recorded.

3. Class discussion can help clarify words, phrases, and ideas. The ten most important concerns can be rank ordered.

4. A rating scale from 0 (Not Serious) to 5 (Very Serious) is placed beside each of the ten top items. This will provide the class with a survey form.

5. Class members then rate the items based on their personal knowledge or opinions. A composite score for each item might then be determined.

6. Next, class members interview groups of students in the school, perhaps by different grade levels, asking them to also rate the same items. Teachers and administrators might rate the items. Thus, a comprehensive survey from representative groups in the school can provide a data based needs assessment. This assessment can then be used to develop peer facilitator projects.

Key Questions:

How are your perceptions different or the same than others in the class? Were you surprised by some of the items which appeared on the list or by the ratings given them? How do you think the data could be used?

Activity 7.2
Mission Possibles

Purpose: To examine problem moments which might occur during a peer facilitator project.

Materials: None

Procedures:

1. Examine the problem moments described below. What would you do in each of the situations?

   a. The student with whom you are tutoring is withdrawn and says very little.

   b. Two buddies in one of your small group sessions are sharing private remarks, making faces to each other, and disrupting the group discussion.

   c. One student in your group is being very domineering, talking constantly, and trying to answer every question that is asked. Others in the group are growing weary.

   d. Your "special friend" has just revealed to you a threat to runaway from home, claiming that parents are too demanding and nagging.

   e. You have been tutoring a student who likes to meet with you but does not follow through with assignments or turn them in to teachers. When confronted, the reply is "It won't make any difference, I'm going to fail anyway."

   f. You are leading a small group discussion when one of the group members becomes sad, begins to cry, and says, "I think I'm addicted to diet pills. It's really beginning to get to me. But, I don't know what to do."

2. The class will discuss the situations in terms of a) What is the person feeling? b) How do you think a peer facilitator might be feeling at the moment? c) What course of action would you recommend and what might be said?

Key Questions:

Are there any other situations which concern you? What would be your first response to the person? Who are some resource people with whom you might consult? When and how do you refer someone for professional help? Is there anything else that you need to be ready to help others?

Chapter 8

The Prevention of School Disorientation

Education is big business in the United States. About 2.5 million teachers will be working with 42.5 million students in public elementary and secondary schools by 1993-94. In addition, the count of private school students is expected to rise to 5.6 million. No matter which school or community, students must learn to adjust and to get the most benefit from their school experiences. When students are disoriented, there is a lack of direction. They feel confused and separate from their classmates and teachers. They lose their bearings and drift away from the purpose of going to school.

A Place Called School

Schools may be in different geographical places, but students across the nation share many of the same needs, interests, and concerns. From one school to the next, you can see similar designs and fads in clothes and hear familiar music or words. Some of the same kinds of social events take place and students talk about many of the same things. Likewise, there are many common problems.

With few exceptions, you can usually recognize a school when you see one. It is a huge, rambling building where hundreds of people meet to study and to learn academic knowledge and skills. It is also a place for social meetings, where people see their friends. A closer look reveals rooms with desks, chalkboards, overhead projectors, and colorful banners and posters. But, what really makes schools different from one another is the way in which people work together and the atmosphere which is created by the working relationships.

Because there are so many people involved, school rules and procedures are needed. Most students find policies helpful, accepting them as part of being in school. Others misunderstand and experience them as too confining or restrictive. Some students have problems adjusting to school, which results in conflicts with teachers, administrators, and other students. These disruptive students complain that school personnel and classmates are insensitive and uncaring. They feel alienated, often preferring not to be in class or school.

There are some students who like school but who lose sight of their goals. They have little interest in learning and find no value in attending class or studying. They often lack the attitude and skills needed to achieve academically. For them, school is primarily a place to meet friends. It is a social gathering. They tolerate going to class in order to be around others their age and to be part of the social scene.

Other students have a more complete understanding and are better adjusted. They grasp the meaning of school, work at developing their skills, and try to gain more knowledge about the world, themselves, and others. They like to socialize, too. School is fun for them and they take in stride the same demands which upset others. They frequently have the same interests and concerns that all other students have and which come with growing up, but they have learned how to adapt and to get the most from school.

Are you one of those students who has learned to adjust and to benefit from school? Or, are you often in conflict with others, perhaps wondering how school is relevant to you? What help did you receive in learning about and adjusting to school? What help did you need or want? What is still missing?

Orientation Programs and School Adjustment

School adjustment depends on a number of things. It helps if there is an organized orientation program to familiarize students with school policies, academic requirements, and general procedures. An effective orientation involves more than giving information. It also includes time for examples, questions, discussion, and follow-up.

Orientation programs acquaint students with school and general expectations. These programs can be for the entire student body or they can focus on different groups with special needs and interests. They can be informative and also offer understanding and support.

New students

New students need help. There are beginning students who are in transition from one grade level to another, perhaps from a middle school to a high school. There are also transfer students who have been attending another school at the same grade level, perhaps from another country, state, or community. New student orientation programs are designed to promote school adjustment.

The goal of these programs is to help students feel secure in a new setting and to provide them with the information needed to be successful. Such programs can feature visits to new schools, talks by counselors, teachers, and older students, and conferences with parents. Sometimes information is presented which may have

little meaning because new students have not yet encountered a situation where they need it. Follow-up and timely suggestions are valuable.

Although adults think they have some good suggestions on how to get along with others, it is too often from their perspective and, even though well intended, may ignore some of the most pressing concerns which students may have. For example, two counselors and four teachers met with a large group of new students in a cafeteria and talked about the school handbook. They described a typical school day. The students, meanwhile, sat patiently and listened. In a short time they became restless, especially as the presentations moved toward describing required credits, course selections, and discipline procedures. The questions on the students' minds were: "Will I be in a class where I know somebody?" "What if I don't like my teachers?" "Where do you go if you have a problem?" "Are the kids going to make fun of me?" "What's the name of the person sitting over there?" "How is this school different?" "Will I like it here?" "Will I be successful?"

Another problem with most orientation programs is that they are often one-time events, usually at the beginning of the school year, or as a part of spring orientation and new campus visits. Because orientation is not on-going during the school year, some students continue to feel disoriented, confused, or still not adjusted. They need more timely assistance, perhaps from someone their own age who understands what they are experiencing.

Some middle and senior high schools have teacher-advisor programs (TAP) where a small group of students (18-22) are assigned one teacher who meets with them as their advisor. Meeting regularly, there are opportunities for advisor and advisees to get to know one another and to receive assistance when appropriate. There are also school counselors who can help, talking with students privately about various issues.

School success skills

Some students need to think about and to learn skills related to school success (e.g. study habits or adjusting to teacher expectations). There are some students who want to change and to get a fresh start, but they are saddled with inappropriate work habits or attitudes. Some of these students have given up and they resist adjusting. Some fail because they do not have appropriate skills and have concluded wrongly that they are failing because they are not smart or cannot learn.

Other students need help in adjusting to school after a prolonged illness and absence. They need help in catching up. A little extra tutoring from a peer helper can make a difference.

There is some evidence that schools with smaller classes have students who learn more and learn easier. There is more interaction between teacher and students and among classmates. But, this may not be a panacea, especially if students lack skills in how to listen, how to take notes, how to organize and start their homework, how to get information if they are unsure of their assignments.

Peervention— What Peers Can Do

Peer helpers can meet with students who have a negative attitude about school. Sometimes individual conferences help where ideas and feelings can be explored. A peer helper does not lecture, reprimand, or threaten others about changing their attitudes. On the contrary, if any change is going to take place, it must be the responsibility of the student who is having trouble in school. However, a friendly talk in which the helper asks some thoughtful questions might encourage the person to think about appropriate attitudes and behaviors.

Some students with negative attitudes about school can be confronted in a friendly way through small group discussions. Structured group activities in which group members talk about themselves and their interests can be productive. Group members think about how others, including their teachers, might see them. Then, they think about how their behaviors affect others. One peer helper said to a student who was having problems with two of his teachers: "How would they describe you and what do you do that would make them say those things?" As the student talked and explored the issues, some ideas surfaced which made the idea of change more meaningful.

Disruptive students who have been referred to the school office for discipline can be targeted for special assistance by peers. Sometimes these students, fearing criticism, resist talking with adults, no matter how well intended they might be. These students need an opportunity to vent their feelings, to explore the consequences of their actions, and to learn new ways of adjusting to school policies and procedures.

High school peer helpers worked with a group of disruptive third graders, who were identified by their teachers as having failed to adjust to school. A planned small group intervention, based on six meetings, was designed and implemented by teams of peer helpers. Two helpers, working together as co-leaders, met with three disruptive third graders. Some group activities involved the children drawing pictures of themselves and situations in school. They talked about how others might describe them and ways to get along with others, including one specific change about themselves which they wanted to make.

In addition, some schools have peer facilitator programs in which peer helpers work with teachers and counselors to help new students feel more positively about school. A counselor or teacher-advisor might present some information and then divide the group into smaller groups, led by peer facilitators, for discussion. The assigned helpers might summarize some of the most important ideas, concerns, or feelings that emerge. These, in turn, might be addressed by the adult leaders when everyone is back in the large group.

Sometimes a peer facilitator is assigned as a "special friend" to a new student. They tour the school, talk about school procedures, make introductions to other students and teachers, and maybe eat lunch together.

In one school, a "support group" of new students met Friday afternoons. This group was led by a school counselor, with the assistance of peer facilitators. Depending on the size of the support group, the peer helpers were assigned to a smaller group (about 3 to 4 new students) and encouraged members to talk about their school experiences: What did you like best about this week at school? What did you like least? What change would need to take place next week in order to make our school better for you? Next, common themes and central issues were summarized by the peer group leaders in front of the large group and this gave the counselor an opportunity to respond and contribute more information. The group typically met for four sessions. Any new students who continued to have concerns or to have trouble adjusting were referred to their respective teacher-advisors or counselors.

Teacher-student relationships are critical in the learning process. Some students need an opportunity to think about how they relate with teachers and how teachers affect them. They need to gain more insight as to how the school day affects their working habits and how even a classroom composed of certain students can affect their willingness to work. Many students want to talk about these important relationships with a trustworthy and friendly person who might understand their circumstances, such as a peer helper.

Summary

Peer facilitators can be the first line of helpers in the schools. As students think aloud about themselves and their problems of adjustment, it may be necessary for peer helpers to refer them to teachers or counselors for additional assistance. In some cases, the peer helper may accompany the student needing help and be present while the student talks with a school counselor or other adult.

Have you ever been in a situation where you were new and did not know others with whom you were grouped? How did you feel? What happened to make things easier for you? Have you ever had a conflict with a teacher or perhaps broken a school rule? How did you feel when confronted? How did you act? What help did you receive and what help would you have liked to have had?

As a peer facilitator, you will have many opportunities to help your classmates and other students to adjust to school. You can take part in some formalized projects which focus on orientation or you may informally show your acceptance and encouragement by being a friendly helper.

Robert D. Myrick and Betsy E. Folk

Activity 8.1
Breaking In and Breaking Out

Purpose:

To experience the feelings and behaviors associated with breaking in and out of groups.

Materials:

None

Procedures:

1. The room is cleared as much as possible, making an open space. All class members stand up and form a large circle. They hold hands, forming a bond. They are designated as a special group.

2. Breaking In: One student volunteers to go first. Standing on the outside of the circle, the student's task is to "break into the inner circle," while others resist. After the first volunteer has tried breaking in, five or six other volunteers attempt the same task.

3. Breaking Out: Next, a different volunteer stands in the middle of the circle and the task is to "break out of the group." After the first volunteer has tried breaking out, five or six other volunteers attempt the same task.

4. All group members who did not volunteer to break in or break out of the group are asked to describe what they saw and heard.

5. Then, the volunteers talk about their experiences of breaking in or out of the group.

6. Finally, the entire group talks about the meaning of the activity as related to school disorientation and student disruption.

Key Questions:

How did people go about breaking in and breaking out of the circle? What strategies did they use? How did others react to the different strategies? Can you think of students in school who are trying to break into a group? Can you think of students who feel trapped and who are trying to break out of a group?

Activity 8.2
Linking the Silence

Purpose:

To experience the feelings and behaviors associated with being part of a group or being isolated and alone.

Materials:

Blindfolds for all group members

Procedures:

1. The room is cleared as much as possible, making an open space. The activity might also be done in a small supervised area outside the classroom.

2. Everyone in the class stands up and puts on a blindfold. Everyone is asked to turn around two times, take two steps forward, and begin saying: *"Peervention."* This is said continuously.

3. The trainer or group leader, who is not blindfolded, is the only one in the room who does not say repeatedly, *"Peervention."*

4. Blindfolded students walk around the room saying *"Peervention"* and trying to find the group leader, who remains silent and will not respond with *"Peervention."*

5. When a blindfolded person finds the group leader, that person takes off the blindfold and joins with the leader and others who may have also found the "quiet one." They join hands to form a quiet group.

6. The blindfolded students continue to call out *"Peervention"* and mill around searching for the silent members, who are standing still together. This process continues until everyone is connected and the entire group is silent.

7. The group then talks about the activity and their experiences.

Key Questions:

How did it feel to be blindfolded and disoriented? How did it feel to call out to others and to link up with the persons you were looking for? What did those students who linked up last experience? What would it be like to be a student who is having trouble linking to others in the school?

Chapter 9

The Prevention of Academic Failure

Although students in American schools are now achieving more in math, science, reading, and writing than those who were in school a few decades ago, many are well below grade level in their studies. Far too many students do not meet reasonable standards for their age.

Some recent data on reading, for example, show that 61% of seventeen-year-olds do not read well enough to understand their assigned textbooks. Almost half cannot understand junior high school mathematics, such as how to find averages. Part of the blame has been given to inappropriate curricula, inadequate teaching, low expectations, lack of school discipline, and a lack of student motivation.

Concern about academic failure and low achievement has spurred state and national governments to legislate changes in schools. Additional graduation requirements, new courses of study, longer school days, and more standardized tests have been mandated. However, there is often a lack of agreement on what ails the schools and what the goals of education should be.

School Dropouts

About 75% of the nation's high school students graduate. After years of frustration and disappointment, 800,000 to 1 million school-age youths give up on their education and dropout of school each year. The dropout percentage in some inner city environments can reach 40% or more.

Dropouts often leave unrecognized and unchallenged, feeling dumb, angry, and neglected. Some are glad to be away from the daily pressure of school life and classrooms where they were made to feel incompetent, inferior, worthless, and alienated by teachers and peers.

Ironically, many school dropouts are able enough to do school work and to be reasonably successful in their classes. In one study of school dropouts, 40% said they had poor relationships with teachers." They put you down," "They don't care," They gave me a hard time." Many felt rejected by teachers and peers and 72% did not talk with any school personnel prior to leaving. More than 70% said that they might have stayed "if teachers had treated us as students and not inmates," and "if school had been more fun." Less than 15% of those surveyed reported that they definitely would not go back. "It's too late for me, I'm too far gone."

How far is too far gone? When does a student lose interest and begin to fail? How many failures does it take before one has no hope and starts doing those things that only make matters worse?

Robert D. Myrick and Betsy E. Folk

Do you know students in your school who have ability but feel mistreated in school? How would teachers describe them? How do teachers work with them? What would it take before these potential dropouts could graduate? What are some of your thoughts and feelings about them?

When asked why they left school, nearly 80% of the dropouts in one study said it was because of problems directly related to the school: a general dislike of the school, feelings of boredom, a sense of not learning anything, problems with teachers, poor test scores and grades, and problems with administrators. "I felt like an outsider." "I felt like I didn't belong." "I didn't drop out, I was pushed out."

For most dropouts, their final decision to leave school is an accumulation of factors or problems. There is a natural progression toward that end because of repeated and unrewarding events, relationships, and circumstances.

There are many factors which can contribute to academic failure and a student's decision to drop out of school. Certainly, poor academic achievement might be one. This is many times related to poor attendance records, truancy, or commitments outside of schools, such as a job or child care. These students often feel hopelessness and suffer from low self-esteem. Many have poor working relationships with teachers and their classmates.

Low Performers

There are some students who may stay in school, but they do not perform well. "Low performing students" or "under-achievers" are students who have the ability or aptitude for learning but have failed to apply themselves. They do not get as much from their classes and studies as they could. These students have more academic potential than what they are realizing.

Sometimes these low performing students lack interest or they feel unmotivated. They may look like they do not have much energy or care about their classes. They are uninvolved and may appear to be lazy. Yet, when they are away from school, they appear to be energized and active in other things. Many of them have events going on in their lives which are distracting and which can keep them from doing better. Some of these students "muddle their way through" with minimal effort because they have other interests and priorities. Some have not applied themselves over a long period of time and have accumulated a deficit in terms of school success skills. Whatever the reason, personal or social, these students fail to put forth their best efforts. They may get by, but in many ways they are failing.

Negative Attitudes

There are some students who have "negative attitudes" which get in the way of learning. They tend to blame others for their problems. They often receive reprimands or discipline reports for failing to go along with school rules and procedures. They argue with teachers, just for the sake of arguing and being unpleasant. They believe that whatever attention is given to them is because they are "tough" and "have a don't care attitude." They assume and expect the worst, often getting what they expected. This, of course, only seems to justify their original negative feelings. They fail to take responsibility for themselves or for their part in the learning process.

It is too easy for them to blame teachers, other students, or their home situations. Their negative attitudes lead to poor teacher and peer relationships. They tend to be disruptive in class and around school. They lack energy and interest in learning. Typically, they do not study or complete their school work and shun anyone who tries to assist them. They are too defensive to ask for help and imagine that others make fun of them. They frequently break school rules and are viewed as uncooperative. This kind of student is difficult to work with but is crying out for help in many ways.

Disadvantaged Students

One group of high risk students in our schools is those who are considered economically or socially disadvantaged. They might be disadvantaged because of such factors as poverty, lack of a family structure, limited English speaking skills, and other socio-economic problems. The number of such disadvantaged students in our nation now stands at about 18.5 million—or more than one third of those who are school-age. And, the number continues to grow.

One estimate was by the year 2000 almost 40% of school-age students will be disadvantaged in some way. And if these new students fare as poorly in school as the ones in school today, the costs in terms of lost wages, reduced tax revenues, increased crime, and additional welfare needs will be staggering. It is very difficult for educationally disadvantaged students to become responsible and productive citizens. The problem is compounded because these same disadvantaged people often become disadvantaged parents to another generation of disadvantaged students. The cycle must be broken. Part of the solution is to prevent academic failure by helping them to learn more, including how to cope with and how to improve their living environments.

Learning Disabled

For many years students with learning disabilities were viewed as unintelligent or slow learners. They often felt discouraged and were frustrated with school, as many of the classroom methods used by teachers were inappropriate for their learning styles. Sadly, many of these same students may have reached the conclusion that they were dumb and unable to learn. Far too many concluded that they should drop out of school.

In the past decade, the number of children labeled as learning disabled (LD) has doubled to about two million. These students have serious difficulties, especially if they are asked to learn in the same way as others who do not have the same problems. For example, a diagnosis may show that a child tends to learn best through the use of visual cues rather than verbal or auditory ones. Other children may need special instruction in reading because of their inability to see the sequential order of some letters. Educators are beginning to rethink their approaches.

The new label of LD or learning disabled has opened the door for some previously low performing students to do better in school and to avoid academic difficulties. These students still need extra attention and can benefit from tutors who help and encourage them with their studies. With help, these students are more hopeful and productive. While learning is still a difficult process, they are beginning to recognize and understand their limitations.

Nevertheless, there are still a great number of LD students who hate school, who hate being labeled a disabled learner, and who hate being out of the mainstream of students. One study of Pittsburgh high schools found a 51% dropout rate for LD students, compared with 32 %for other students.

There is still a need for more research in this area. The effects of labeling people, however, are already obvious. Peer facilitators can assist teachers with special education students through many projects. The students can be encouraged to talk about their experiences and feel supported by peers. Working with peer facilitators is one way to help LD students maintain positive self-concepts.

Who is "At Risk?"

The term "at risk" is used to describe those students who have a high risk of failing and/or leaving school before they graduate. It has also been used to include students who come from disadvantaged homes where learning is not valued or supported, and where it is difficult to achieve because of family or neighborhood conditions.

These students are "at risk" to themselves, to others, and to society. They are at risk to themselves because they will likely lack the skills to help them to get good jobs, to perform well in jobs, or to compete in the job market. They usually become unskilled workers, who are quickly unemployed when economic times are tough. The same lack of attention and desire to learn in school often becomes a characteristic that shows up in jobs outside of school.

They are, therefore, a high risk to our nation. Our society is changing. There is a need for more skilled workers. Technological advances are displacing approximately one million unskilled workers each year. While manufacturing jobs decline, there are growing opportunities in the service industries (i.e. sales, tourism, marketing, and communications). However, the skills necessary to succeed in these growing fields are the very same skills that most "at risk" students lack.

At risk students are a high risk to other students. Too often at risk students tend to disrupt the learning process in schools. They distract others. They keep teachers from giving attention to those who want to learn. They make the learning climate unpleasant. Because they have little or no interest in their studies, they attempt to get attention by doing things that are counter productive. They make inappropriate remarks and noises. They try to get teachers and classmates off task. They make fun of those who are more interested in school and who are trying to study. They present a risk to any student who is easily influenced by their behavior and attitudes and who feels intimidated.

Peervention— ## What Peers Can Do

Some at risk students lack the basic skills to help them learn. They do not know how to study. They cannot spell or write well. They do not read well. They often fall behind in school and fail to complete class assignments. Helping them learn and practice basic school success skills might be a place to start.

Peer facilitators can help prevent academic failure by creatively tutoring high risk students in learning skills. A skills unit might be developed which could be led by peers. At risk students have not responded well to traditional approaches where they are labeled and isolated and then told to move at a slower pace because they are behind in their work. This may have the opposite effect on students, making them feel neglected and less able.

On the contrary, what is needed is an approach that will focus on a student's strengths rather than highlight weaknesses. They do *not* need more boring drill and skill lessons. They *do* need more opportunities to participate in a variety of cooperative learning projects where they can work with other students who model skills for them. They need encouragement more than criticism. Studying is more interesting when they are actively involved and feel supported.

Most of the at risk students can benefit from both individual and group study sessions. Peer tutoring can be directly related to class assignments, such as learning how to write a paragraph. It can also be indirectly related to the assignment by having students manage a school store where they have to write a letter and apply the skill. A student can learn to read by using either school literature books or popular magazines, even comic books. A student can learn to do math assigned either in a textbook or through a computer game where calculations are needed in order to win. Students can study classic poems or examine popular song lyrics, as a way of understanding principles of poetry. There is more than one way to learn an idea or concept.

Community outreach projects are interesting, but they require liaison work between school and community agencies. Can this be done by trained peer facilitators? Some peers might be able to help others understand their neighborhoods and discover how changes might be made. These same peers might also help others learn of the strengths of such a community and how these strengths can be drawn upon.

For instance, one young girl, Maria, lived in a neighborhood that was primarily Spanish-speaking and made up of several disadvantaged families. Many of the parents were limited in their English skills. Even though they wanted their children to do well in school, they felt inadequate in helping them with homework. The parents also felt like outsiders to the school because of their poor communication skills. Maria was torn between two kinds of environments, but because she was bilingual, she was a valuable resource. With peer facilitator training, she worked as a liaison between some parents and school officials. As a peer helper, she met new students, especially those with limited English skills, and introduced them to the school. She also worked as a facilitator when teachers and students had trouble communicating or understanding one another.

Summary

All of the four peer facilitator roles can be used in projects related to the prevention of academic failure. Remember, you are not expected to be responsible for the behavior of those who are neglectful of their studies or who act out against the school. You cannot make decisions for others. But, you can say and do things that will help your peers to think about their actions, to consider alternatives, to practice skills, and to enjoy school. You can offer them timely support.

Robert D. Myrick and Betsy E. Folk

Activity 9.1
Messages People Wear

Purpose:

To increase awareness of how at risk students are influenced by the messages they give people and the responses they in turn receive. To recognize how labeling students can affect attitudes and behaviors.

Materials:

Cards or slips of paper with role labels and messages, transparent tape

Procedures:

1. The room is cleared as much as possible, making an open space.

2. Everyone in the class draws a role card and tapes it to the forehead of another class member, making sure that person cannot see what is written on the card. Do not tell anyone what is on their cards.

3. After all of the participants have a role card and message taped to their foreheads, the game begins. Remind them not to take the cards off their heads until the game is completed.

4. Ten minutes is allotted for everyone to mill around the room and respond to each other according to the messages taped on the foreheads. During this time, make an effort to interact with as many people as you can.

5. After time is called by the group leader, take a seat. Your card remains on your head.

6. Each person now takes a turn and shares how it felt to wear the message and guesses what the message says.

7. Discuss the activity and experience with the class.

Key Questions:

What messages were the easiest to respond to? The most difficult? How did you feel when people looked at your message and immediately responded in certain ways? Did their responses give you any clues as to the message you were wearing?

Did you receive any mixed messages? Can you think of students or groups of students whose actions give a loud message about themselves and the kind of response they hope to receive?

Can you think of other roles and messages which students in your school often give?

Labels and Messages

Role 1:   I am Intelligent.

Message: Ask me anything.

Role 2:   I am Attractive.

Message: Look at me and notice me.

Role 3:   I am Fragile.

Message: Treat me gently.

Role 4:   I am Angry.

Message: Be threatened by me.

Role 5:   I am Boring.

Message: Ignore me.

Role 6:   I am Irritating.

Message: Be careful what you say to me.

Role 7:   I am Argumentative.

Message: Yell or argue with me.

Role 8:   I am Insecure.

Message: Support me.

Role 9:   I am Failing.

Message: Help me.

Role 10:   I am Different.

Message: Prove you can be trusted.

Role 11:   I am an Underachiever.

Message: Remind me how dumb I am.

Role 12:   I am a Loner.

Message: Leave me alone.

Activity 9.2
Feedback and Failure

Purpose:

To practice giving feedback (compliments and confrontations) to at risk students who are in danger of failing.

Materials:

None

Procedures:

1. Using the vignettes below, write a feedback (confrontation or compliment) response which you might use as a response to the student.

2. Next, join a group of four. In turn, tell what you wrote as a response. Read it as if you were saying it to the person. After all group members have shared their responses, move to the next vignette and again tell what each of you wrote.

3. Decide among yourselves which response, or combination of responses, that you would try to use if you were in that situation.

4. If time permits, each group of four will share the response which they recommend.

Key Questions:

What did you consider when writing your feedback response? What kind of impact do you think your response and the responses of others in your group could make? When might be the best time to make such a response? What else could you do or say when confronting or complimenting?

Feedback Vignettes

1. Sara thought she was going to drop out of school. She was discouraged. However, she met with you and agreed to manage her time better so that she could complete more of her class assignments. She recently joined the Beta Club, which provided service to the school and where she met a new friend. Sara said, "I have decided to stay in school. Thanks for listening to me when I was down." GIVE SARA A COMPLIMENT!

2. Shawn makes fun of other students. He tends to be sarcastic and puts down students who are in special classes. He calls them "The Weirdos" and makes faces when he talks about them. Shawn thinks his remarks are clever and funny. You notice that some students are staying clear of him. CONFRONT SHAWN!

3. Mario does not speak English well. He is self-conscious about his accent and avoids participating in class. He is afraid students will make fun of him and prefers to remain aloof and silent. One teacher says that Mario could get better grades in class, but he must take part in more of the class discussions. You like Mario and have some unpleasant feelings regarding his situation. CONFRONT MARIO!

4. Kim is part of a large single-parent family with limited financial resources. She has a lot of responsibilities at home, including taking care of her younger brothers and sisters. This prevents her from being involved in after school activities and going places with friends. Kim attends school regularly, is cheerful, has a friendly smile, and completes her school work. She listens carefully to others talk about their problems, but rarely complains about her own. COMPLIMENT KIM!

Robert D. Myrick and Betsy E. Folk

Chapter 10

The Prevention of Depression and Suicide

Are you a racehorse or a turtle? If you are a racehorse, then you may find it hard to stand still at the gate. You can hardly wait until the bell sounds and you rush to the finish line. Your life is full of activities. Some racehorses are so distracted that they must wear blinders around their eyes in order to move straight ahead. They anxiously pound the ground with their hooves and then charge off with explosive energy. Everyone admires the drive and ambition of the racehorse.

Turtles obviously move at a much slower pace. They, too, can move toward a finish line. But, their movement suggests that they are less frenzied and less anxious to begin the race. If you are a turtle, then you may take fewer risks, prefer the comfort of your shell, and wonder why others are rushing around you. However, the turtle knows that you can only make progress by sticking your neck out.

Both turtles and racehorses have their own unique style of racing through life. Both must protect themselves at times. And both experience stress. It is easier to see the anxiety, sweat, and uncertainty of the racehorse who is in front of the crowd. Yet, the same kinds of stress may be experienced by the turtle, but it is not as visible because of the turtle's shell.

Managing the Stress of Life

Everyone experiences stress. Stress can be helpful. It can spur you to move toward a goal. It can alert you to dangerous situations and make you cautious. It can stimulate your thinking and encourage you to find solutions to problems. When stress is managed well, it can assist both racehorses and turtles to be successful.

Stress can be destructive when it is not managed well or when it becomes excessive. People who are "stressed out" have trouble concentrating and often feel exhausted or fatigued. Because they feel anxious, their hearts pump fast, their breathing speeds up, and they may develop nervous habits. Prolonged stress can lead to serious illness.

An overly stressful turtle may become a "snapping" turtle. It is irritable, restless, and may tremble. It is not always easy to see the effects of stress in some turtles because they retreat within their shells. An overly stressful racehorse may seem bad tempered, moody, and unpredictable. It may become aggressive or apathetic.

Are you a racehorse or a turtle? While this may help you identify your general style in coping with life, perhaps the more important question is, how much stress do you carry with you while running the race?

None of us lives a stress free life. Excessive stress with some people has led to accidents, emotional outbursts, over-eating or loss of appetite, and dependency on drugs. Excessive stress has also been linked to forgetfulness, poor decision making, impulsive actions, nervous laughter, and inadequate relationship with others. Therefore, each of us needs to develop skills in managing stress.

Four Kinds of Stress

There are four basic kinds of stress in our lives. The first one is ***developmental***. Certain stages of your life are more stressful than others. The first day of school is stressful for a lot of children. Trying out for team sports or asking someone for a date can be stressful. Moving from one school to another produces some anxious moments. Almost all individuals are nervous when they have to take tests or give speeches in front of their classes. It can be stressful to think about and make plans for life after graduation from high school.

Being a teenager is a stressful time of life. This is a period of development when relationships become "stressors." There is pressure to get along with teachers, to have special friendships with boys and girls, to resolve conflicts with parents, and to meet the expectations of others.

Adolescents are very aware of their peer groups. They are sensitive to the reactions of others. They want to be independent and self-reliant, but are still dependent on their families. The issue of sexuality can be very stressful for teens as some feel the need to experiment, to prove themselves, or to act cool, as if they understood all the mysteries of life.

The second kind of stress is ***environmental***. This stress is caused by everyday encounters. When driving your car in traffic you may find yourself angry that the light just turned red . It is almost as if it changed deliberately to get you. Some students find school a stressful place to be, full of flashing red lights warning them what not to do. The home environment, with responsibilities or a lack of them, may be more stressful than nourishing.

The teenage years also bring an increased amount of peer pressure. This pressure is often related to the environment in which students live and go to school. Some young people feel peer pressure to use alcohol and other drugs. Some mistakenly think that alcohol and drugs will help them escape from environmental stress.

The third kind of stress is **physical**. Changes in your body can create moments of anxiety or tension, such as a woman's drop in hormonal level each month just before menstruation. A young man may notice that his voice has not changed as it has with some of his peers. Physical changes among adolescents also lead to increased thoughts about sexuality. Some of these changes create tense and uncertain moments.

Many people learn relaxation techniques in order to help them reduce tension. They may be involved in some aerobic exercise to maintain good health. Without exercise, the body can become sluggish and ineffective. When the body does not function well, it harbors more stress and works like a squeaky machine that can break down at any moment. Excessive physical stress can lead to ulcers, headaches, and frequent fatigue. Although the proper amount of stress can create a feeling of physical well-being, excessive physical stress can be damaging.

A fourth kind of stress is **psychological.** What is stressful for one person may not be stressful for another. A lot of stress can be related to how people perceive a situation and the kind of psychological impact that it has on them. For example, a student who is prepared for a test may be less anxious than one who is not. One the other hand, the person who is prepared for the test may place more importance on test results and worry about the outcome. Another student may not care about the results and simply go through the motions of taking the test. The psychological meaning of an event or situation can determine the degree of stress the person must manage.

People who are unable to manage stress in their lives eventually experience letdowns and low levels of energy. Excessive stress eventually causes withdrawal in order to psychologically survive. Without help, this stress can result in depression and dangerous risks to life.

Depression

"I'm tired." "I don't feel like doing anything." "I just want to be alone." Have you ever found yourself just feeling blue? Depression afflicts approximately six million Americans under the age of eighteen each year. Depression is a common psychological complaint.

Depression can range from feeling very sad and lonely to having thoughts of self-destruction. Depression can be brief or prolonged. It can be triggered by a single event or a persistent problem. It might result from a vague feeling of helplessness which has continued over an extended period of time.

Sara is a middle school student. She scores well on tests and is generally liked by her peers. However, her physical maturity is somewhat delayed and she is self-conscious about her physical development. She is embarrassed to take showers in physical education class, and has on occasion been teased about being tall and "skinny." One of her friends noticed that she seemed distant and avoided going places, especially when boys were around. Sara's energy level was low and her absences from school increased. Rather than take part in school activities, she chose to sit at home and watch television. She became less communicative. She was depressed.

Loss

Loss is a major contributor to depression. Losing something of value can create excessive stress. Can you recall times when you have lost something important? Perhaps it was a favorite ring or piece of clothing. When you were younger, it may have been a favorite toy. These are anxious and sad moments, especially when you realize that you cannot recover them.

For teenagers, the loss of a boy friend or girlfriend can be traumatic. Such a loss may spin a person into a fit of depression. When Kevin and Stacy broke up with each other after dating for a long time, Stacy was obsessed with the loss. She talked about it incessantly. She cried. She swore. She worried that her life was ruined and could not imagine living without Kevin. When it became obvious that the close relationship was lost, she even talked of dying. Her friends were concerned that her depression was making her do some irrational things.

The loss of a parent through divorce or death often brings sadness. Left unchecked, the sadness may lead to depression. Divorce and death change relationships. A young person may not have any control over the circumstances and subsequently feel helpless and depressed. While time can be a great healer, those who have experienced the loss of a loved one can benefit from talking with others about what they are experiencing.

Ellis was a senior who looked forward to entering a technological school after graduation. He wanted to learn more about computers and aircraft mainte- nance. Then, unexpectedly, his father died in an accident. The family was thrown into personal and financial problems. His younger brothers and sisters needed his support and he realized that he would have to get a job in order to assist the family. Ellis saw his hopes and dreams for going to college begin to disappear. He was experiencing a loss of options. Even though he was admired for helping out his family and caring for his siblings, Ellis seemed burdened with hopelessness and eventually needed counseling because of his depression.

Taking drugs or drinking alcohol can make people depressive. After the initial high or stimulation, there is always a come down. For some people, the let down is more of a crash and frequently results in a heavy depression. A recent study showed that many adolescents admitted to a hospital following a suicide attempt had traces of drugs in their urine. Substances such as alcohol and other drugs have a depressant effect which lowers resistance and magnifies feelings of loneliness, isolation, sadness, loss, and depression.

Other causes of depression attributed to teenagers include: physical, emotional, or sexual abuse; overwhelming shame or guilt; a rapid loss of self-esteem; peer rejection; lack of school success; and lacking a purpose and direction in life. Some studies have shown that young people who often experience depression typically have parents who also struggle with depression. These children need assistance in learning to be independent and responsible for their own well-being. They may need more positive models and timely support during stressful times.

Temporary depression can be normal for teens. They are going through a lot of physical and emotional changes in becom- ing a young adult. They are also bom- barded with opportunities and choices. Teenagers are still learning about them- selves and others which is fraught with highs and lows, ups and downs, and uncertainties. However, when there is a persistence of low feelings regarding self- worth, self-confidence, or self-acceptance, these are warning signals that must be heeded.

Suicide

Deep depression can drive people to self destruction. The occurrence of suicide among teenagers has doubled over the past ten years and now ranks second only to accidents as the leading cause of death for the age group 11-24. Even many accidents are thought to be disguised suicides.

It is estimated that 7,000 teenagers kill themselves each year, and at least ten times that number attempt to kill themselves. The estimated number may be as high as 500,000 per year since many attempts go unreported.

For every successful teenage suicide attempt there are 50 to 100 self destructive acts which do not result in death. One third of the adolescents who survive these acts attempt to take their life again within two years. It has also been noted that 90% of teen suicide attempts take place in the home between 3:00 P.M. and midnight.

These are startling and horrifying statistics. What anxiety or torment must many young people be experiencing to feel that the only solution is death? It becomes important for each of us to become aware of the signs and symptoms of depression and suicide.

A suicide pact by four sisters who took rat poison so their parents could afford to take care of their brother sent shock waves through a community in Korea in 1989. They were poor and they wanted to ensure that their three-year-old brother, in a society dominated by men, was able to have the best education.

A friendly, high achieving fifteen-year-old boy, who was an Eagle Scout, stood up in his English class, pulled a .38 caliber gun from his clothing, pointed it at his head, and fired. His death was a mystery.

Unfortunately, there is no easily recognizable suicidal type. No single group, race, religion, or class is exempt from depression or suicidal death. Suicide appears to be divided equally among all socio-economic groups. There are many myths about young people who are depressed and suicidal.

Myths

1. **If you talk about it, you will not do it.** This is one of the most commonly believed myths. Research suggests that all suicidal teenagers make attempts (either verbal or nonverbal) to let a parent, friend, or teacher know that life is becoming too unbearable. Suicide is a desperate cry for help. It is of course, the poorest of all options. It is final and threats need to be taken seriously. One should never assume that a statement such as, "I do not want to live anymore" is an idle treat or only being used to attract attention.

2. **It is just a stage and it will pass.** While it might be true that some people might have suicidal thoughts at different times or stages of their lives which they do not act on, suicide is not a stage of life. Obsessive thoughts of self-destruction are not typical and should not be dismissed as something everybody goes through.

3. **Suicide happens with no warning.** In reality, suicidal adolescents often leave numerous hints and warning regarding their intentions. They provide a lot of clues. For example, they may become increasingly dependent on sleeping pills, pain-relieving drugs, alcohol, or illegal substances. They may become accident prone. They may be unusually attracted to stories about death and violence, perhaps speculating how they would carry out such an act. They may pull away from friends and classmates, parents and teachers, making it more difficult for others to notice warning signs.

4. **Suicide is hereditary.** Suicide is an inappropriate solution to stress that often occurs as a possibility in some families. The emotional climate in some families and neighborhoods increases the risk that its members are exposed to suicidal attempts. This is also true for physical and sexual abuse. However, there is no evidence to indicate that it is genetic. More importantly, it seems that suicide is often a response to stress in a person's environment.

Robert D. Myrick and Betsy E. Folk

Warning signs

A number of experts believe that nine out of ten adolescents who complete suicide give advanced cues to those around them. It is important to recognize these signs and symptoms in order to be of help. Here are some typical signals.

1. **A lack of concern for safety and personal welfare**—Reckless driving, accepting dares from friends, lack of personal hygiene, are all possible signs of someone who is saying, "I am hurting, and do not care about myself."

2. **Breaking social patterns**—Unusual or sudden changes in an adolescent's behavior may suggest that the person is feeling desperate. For instance, a teenager may suddenly start arguing intensely with parents or siblings, breaking rules, or retreating to the bedroom in order to avoid others. While adolescents love to sleep in, a warning sign may be when they show signs of excessive fatigue and apathy.

3. **Decline in school achievement**—Adolescents who are preoccupied with suicidal thoughts do not give attention to their school work. They fail to complete homework assignments, and their grades suffer.

4. **A lack of clear and logical thinking**—Suicidal persons have trouble thinking logically. Their problem solving ability is impaired because of stress and depression. It is difficult for them to concentrate on positive matters and they may become obsessed with a "final" solution. Sometimes their thinking may be disjointed and they may be unable to carry on a rational conversation.

Troubled adolescents may turn to alcohol or other drugs in order to lessen their discontent. They may feel that a "drug" increases their feelings of self-esteem. Unfortunately, it may only serve to deceive them. Under the influence of alcohol or drugs, thinking patterns can become distorted, impulse control lessened, and personal identity is lost.

Still other warning signs include:

- Change in eating or sleeping patterns
- Remarks about worthlessness or desire for death
- Giving away personal possessions
- Deep and prolonged grief over any loss
- Negative "self-talk"

Some signals or warnings are difficult to identify. Some signals are loud and clear. When any individuals express a desire to die, or threaten to kill themselves, it is important to take them seriously. They need help.

Peervention— **What Peers Can Do**

When assisting these very depressed young people, there seems to be universal agreement on the manner in which to help them. The helper needs to be non-judgmental, to treat the young person's problems seriously, and to ask direct questions. The helper also needs to communicate support and concern. Being a trained listener and facilitator is an important way in which to help distressed young people.

The suicidal person should not be left alone if the threat seems immediate. An appropriate person such as a counselor, concerned teacher, or other health care professional should be contacted. As a peer facilitator, you may be working with young people who present signs of being depressed or suicidal. It is important for you to take the necessary steps to ensure their safety. You should notify your sponsor or leader immediately if you have any concerns about another student's safety or well-being.

As a peer facilitator, you may want to offer students other options to decrease their feelings of depression. You may invite them to accompany you to a ball game, or meet at the mall for a Saturday afternoon. Exploring options is an important way a peer facilitator can assist those who are in a state of depression.

Knowledge of appropriate referral agencies is essential. The peer facilitator can give a depressed student the number of a local hotline or crisis center. In addition, peer facilitators can volunteer their own time and services to a hotline or crisis center. These are over 200 hotlines in communities throughout our country.

Other prevention efforts that peer facilitators may be involved in are conducting stress management workshops for young people. These workshops could focus on awareness building of signs and signals of stress, depression, and suicide. Parent education workshops, with time built in for honest discussions, are also an option for peer facilitators. These can be organized and offered in the evenings at schools.

Student helpers can organize support groups on their campus for students who need an opportunity to share their concerns and feelings. In addition, student helpers might become instrumental members of crisis teams on their own campus.

According to one survey, 93% of the students reported that they would turn to a friend before anyone else in a crisis. Although a teacher, a minister, a rabbi, a neighbor, or a professional counselor can provide special assistance and may need to be consulted, depressed youth almost always turn first to their peers for help.

Robert D. Myrick and Betsy E. Folk

Activity 10.1
The Stress Box

Purpose:

To increase awareness of factors which contribute to stress and unhappiness.

Materials:

Paper, large box

Procedures:

1. Think of three things which cause you personal stress or make you sad. Write each one on separate pieces of paper.

2. A large box is placed in the middle or front of the room, where everyone can see and reach it.

3. In turn, share with the group one of the items from the list. Explain briefly why the item causes you discomfort and other unpleasant feelings.

4. After you have told about the item, get rid of this stress by wadding up the paper, tossing it in the box, and saying something assertive such as, "You're out of here."

5. Listen as a group member describes a stressful item. If you have written something similar, then when it comes time to throw the item into the box, join in and follow the person to the box, throwing your own item in too, and repeating the same assertive statement.

6. Then, another person in the group shares a different stress point or event. Follow the same procedures as before.

7. The process continues until all items have been shared and thrown away.

Key Questions:

Which stressful items did most of the group seem to have? What emotions did you hear as people talked about the stress? How did it feel to throw the stressful item into the box? What steps can you take to actually reduce or throw away the stress items you listed?

Activity 10.2
The Gloomy, Doomy Mural

Purpose:

To increase awareness of factors which contribute to depression and suicidal tendencies.

Materials:

Paper for a large mural, colored crayons or markers

Procedures:

1. A mural paper is placed on a writing surface, perhaps the floor, a table, or wall. The paper is divided into equal sections, one for each student in the class. Each student is also given a black or brown colored marker or crayon.

2. In your space draw a design or symbol which illustrates one or more reasons that you think contributes to teenagers' depression and attempts at suicide.

3. When everyone is finished, group members take turns telling about their designs and reactions to the designs drawn by others.

4. The group identifies and discusses the factors which contribute to teenage depression and attempts at suicide.

5. Next, the group brainstorms things which could be done to help prevent depression and suicidal tendencies.

6. Then, using bright colored crayons or markers, all class members go to their spaces on the mural and quickly draw symbols and pictures representing the helping strategies and ideas. These may be drawn over or on top of the dark designs and symbols.

Key Questions:

Which of the negative factors discussed in class do you think are most likely to be present in your school? Community? Was it helpful to see the dark side of depression and suicide presented visually? What difference, if any, did it make to brighten the mural with prevention strategies?

Chapter 11

The Prevention of Eating Disorders

We cannot ignore the fact that many people in our nation go hungry at night and are unsure where or when they will get their next meal. However, the vast majority of people have plenty to eat and rather than worry about starving, they worry about putting or pounds or taking them off. Americans have become weight watchers.

Medical studies recommend that we should eat balanced meals and that it is wise to pay attention to foods and their effects on us. "We are what we eat," said one expert. If you eat a lot of fatty foods, then you are likely to put on extra pounds unless you can exercise enough to burn up the excess calories. Far too many people have formed poor eating habits early in life and now are faced with eating problems. The word "diet" has become a common place word in everyday conversations.

There have been all kinds of fad diets: The Grapefruit Diet; The Immune Power Diet; the Scarsdale Diet; and others. A nation of 65 million dieters has tried them all, many times moving from one to another. Knowing that so many people are weight conscious, advertisers flood us with television commercials and remind us how much happier we will be after we have lost weight by using their products.

Americans tend to look for quick and easy fixes when they are in trouble. For example, last year 20 million Americans spent nearly one billion dollars on liquid diets, hoping to change their body images with a few weeks of semi-starvation. Ironically, as many as half of the people who sign up for medically supervised diet programs never finish them. Even those who lose weight are three times more likely to regain it than those who take off pounds more slowly.

Being weight conscious, of course, is related to living a healthy life. It makes sense to have good eating habits and many of these habits are formed early in life. In addition, people are physically different. Some have metabolism rates, by birth, that enable them to consume large quantities of food and burn up the calories in the normal course of a day. Others, at an early age, learn that their body stores fat quickly and that it is easy to put on extra pounds without eating very much.

Being weight conscious is also related to our self-images in social situations. Being slender and in good physical condition is a standard by which most people judge others, whether or not they themselves are trim and fit. It is a standard that has become accepted because it is a media image. Models on television who wear clothes, bathing suits, drive cars, or talk about products are people who clearly watch their figures. Almost everyone judges themselves by the same standards of perfection, many of which are unrealistic. Nevertheless, they appeal to us and we often aspire to match them.

The Body Image

Eating, dieting, controlling weight, and exercising are related to body image. Sadly, very few people, if any, are content with their bodies Even the most glamorous models worry about their looks, are usually unhappy with certain parts of their bodies, and spend a lot of time thinking about their eating habits and body weight. Their jobs depend on it. Some have developed eating disorders.

Teenagers often find fault with their bodies. The nose is too big. The eyes are not the right color. The hair is too curly or not curly enough. And so on. It is often

Robert D. Myrick and Betsy E. Folk

assumed that if one is slender and physically fit, then social acceptance will follow, including having many friends and being admired by others. Popularity is often related to body appearance, at least initially. Is it any wonder, then, that obsessions with "looking good" and not putting on weight has led to eating disorders?

Anorexia

Anorexia is an eating disorder in which one is constantly preoccupied with how food puts on body weight and is the source of fat. It is more than stringent dieting. The anorexic cannot tolerate the thought of being seen as fat or heavy. The fear of being socially rejected and not meeting one's own standards if overweight becomes an obsession to the point of self-destruction. Thoughts about food are distorted until all food becomes unappetizing.

Girls are ten times more likely than boys to develop this disorder. An anorexic craves food but stubbornly refuses to eat or retain it, preferring to starve to the point of illness, invalidism, and possibly death. Food is an enemy.

Many anorexics are bright, aggressive teenagers. They want to be in control, but in their relentless pursuit of thinness, they actually do the opposite. They lose control over their bodies, destroying body balances and systems, including brain functioning. They may feel hungry, but they will not eat. Ultimately, the most severe anorexics starve themselves to death.

Bulimia

The self-induced or peer pressure to be thin can also lead to bulimia, another eating disorder. Bulimia is a self-destructive method of weight control and involves binging and purging.

Bulimics might regularly gorge themselves with food, especially high caloric food, for periods lasting up to several hours. Then, to avoid gaining weight, they purge themselves through self-induced vomiting and/or laxative and diuretic abuse. Some have estimated that as many as 20% of women in college are bulemic.

People with bulimia differ from anorexics by having normal body weight. Also, bulemics usually recognize that there is something wrong, while anorexics refuse to believe that their behaviors are abnormal.

Eating disorders have reached record proportions in our nation within the last ten years. There are over 500,000 people who are known to be afflicted with this problem. At one time or another, approximately 15 to 25 of every 200 high school girls (7.5% to 12.5%) will be anorexic, bulimic, or on the borderline. In general about two to four boys (1% to 2%) will be bulemic.

Serious medical problems can occur from extreme weight loss, excessive vomiting, and use of laxatives. It may result in the shrinking of internal organs, including the heart, kidneys, and brain. As the heart weakens, it can develop irregular patterns and result in congestive heart failure. Feet and hands frequently get cold and there is a loss of energy. Reproductive organs can also be affected adversely.

Causes and symptoms of eating disorders

Some possible causes of eating disorders have been traced to psychological origins. Some experts believe that a fear of growing up is the root of the problem. Others see it as a rebellion against parents who have set very high standards. All agree that food is not the central issue.

It is possible that biological factors may play an important part. There is some evidence that anorexics, for example, secrete abnormal amounts of various hormones. But, these imbalances may be the result of emotional stress and severe dieting, not the cause of them.

Social pressures, or at least the thought of not being accepted by others, is a major cause of eating disorders. In America, dieting is considered normal behavior. The stress of looking like models on television or in published advertisements weighs heavily on many people's minds.

Some common symptoms are: unusual loss of weight (more than 25%), denial of hunger, absent or irregular menstrual cycle, excessive compulsion to exercise, inability to think clearly, abuse of laxatives or diuretics, depression, or dramatic mood changes. Rapid loss of hair and skin problems may also occur.

Peervention— What Peers Can Do

If you know of some individuals who have an eating disorder, you will want to help them receive medical attention. Professional treatment is probably necessary. You may be the catalyst or key person in the referral process.

The goal is to help people gain control of their lives and to see things more realistically. They need to accept themselves more and to take responsible measures toward good health.

Teresa, a tenth grade student, was losing a lot of weight. She appeared to have lost 20 to 25 pounds and her weight dropped to a total of 85 pounds. She had not had a menstrual cycle for six months. Her family encouraged her to eat, but to no avail. Teresa was on the track team and every day she would run five miles. Her body was depleted and in need of food. The added stress of rigorous running caused Teresa to collapse one day. She was taken to the hospital and diagnosed as anorexic. It took two years and psychological counseling before she regained her proper body weight. She still has trouble concentrating and writing. Some of her friends noticed the loss of weight but were unsure of what to say or do. They may have cared about Teresa but their inability to talk with her about the problem, to confront her, or to get her some help before she collapsed prevented timely assistance.

Peer facilitators are trained to build helping relationships and to reach out to others who may need assistance. They might be in the role of being special friends to others who are worried about their body image and who are starting self-destructive behaviors. The systematic problem solving model might be introduced and gentle confrontations may be appropriate. Sometimes individuals can make better decisions about themselves just knowing that they are accepted and liked.

If the eating disorder persists, then an appropriate referral to a professional helper is in order. You may need to go with the person and help make introductions. You may be the bridge to health.

You might also take part in an educational forum. Prevention of eating disorders might be promoted through discussion groups or classroom presentations. Peer facilitators can participate in projects which help others become aware of warning signals. In this sense, it is also possible to be a part of an early identification system where students are encouraged to examine their problems and causes before they become dangerous and before medical treatment is needed.

Because eating disorders are so closely associated with self-image, self-acceptance, social pressure, and stressful events, you can also be a part of projects which help others learn more about themselves and others. One project might focus on typical causes of stress in teenagers and healthy ways in which to manage anxiety.

Support groups may be of particular help in some schools. A group of students may join together in order to cope with their problems of stress and related eating disorders. They may find comfort in knowing that they are not the only ones who want to gain control and to make changes. Leading a group discussion or helping the group to become better acquainted and to explore the issues through learning activities may be a valuable role for you.

One way to help, which will also benefit yourself, is to be a model to others. Learn about nutrition and make healthy choices in your food selections and eating habits. If you are trying to eat balanced meals on a regular basis, others may take notice and be influenced positively.

Activity 11.1
Food for Thought

Purpose:

To increase awareness of eating habits.

Materials:

Paper and pencil

Procedures:

1. Divide a piece of paper into six equal parts.

2. Draw a picture or symbol to show your answer or response to each of the following questions:

   A. What are your two favorite foods?

   B. Where is a place where you enjoy eating food?

   C. When was a time when you ate too little food?

   D. When was a time when you ate too much food?

   E. What is a food you could easily overeat?

   F. What is a food you would choose not to eat?

3. Form a group of three and discuss the symbols or pictures that you have drawn.

Key Questions

Look at your favorite foods. Are they nutritious or are they junk food? Do you eat them often and are they similar to what other classmates chose?

Look at the place you like to eat: Are you alone or with others? Is it fast paced or slow paced? Do you almost always have the same thing? When you ate too little or too much, were the foods similar? Or different? How did you feel before and after eating? What factors influenced you to eat too much or too little? Are the foods you can easily overeat, or choose not to eat, nutritious or junk food? Are you aware of what you eat, or does it make any difference? What has influenced your likes and dislikes of certain foods?

Activity 11.2
Strategies for Good Health

Purpose:

To increase awareness of prevention strategies related to eating disorders.

Materials:

Paper and pencil

Procedures:

1. On a piece of paper, rate yourself (1 is low and 5 is high) by circling the numbers to the right on the following items:

   In general I....

A.	Eat three well-balanced meals a day.	1	2	3	4	5
B.	Am the proper weight for my age and height.	1	2	3	4	5
C.	Get 7-8 hours of sleep per night.	1	2	3	4	5
D.	Avoid snack foods.	1	2	3	4	5
E.	Tend to choose nutritious food over junk food.	1	2	3	4	5
F.	Exercise on a regular basis.	1	2	3	4	5
G.	Do not use food to cope with stress.	1	2	3	4	5
H.	Avoid taking diet pills.	1	2	3	4	5
I.	Would talk with a professional if I were concerned about my eating habits.	1	2	3	4	5
J.	Control my eating habits rather than their controlling me.	1	2	3	4	5
K.	Can make good food choices even though others around me are not.	1	2	3	4	5
L.	Rarely binge on favorite foods.	1	2	3	4	5

2. Add the numbers circled and look at the following scale to help interpret your score.

Score:

1-15	*Whoa! You are in trouble. Talk with a counselor.*
16-25	*You are making a lot of poor choices. What can you do to become healthier?*
26-35	*You have some poor eating habits. What are they?*
36-45	*You seem to be doing all right. But, what else can you do?*
46-55	*You are on target and health conscious. Congratulations!*
55-60	*Are you in training for the Olympics? Relax and have a cookie. But, share some of your strategies with a friend.*

Key Questions

In a group, without telling your score, talk about which item could you improve on the most? Which one gives you the most difficulty? How satisfied are you with your score? Is it accurate for you? How would you rate others in your family?

Robert D. Myrick and Betsy E. Folk

Chapter 12

The Prevention of Family Distress

The traditional family consists of two married adults—a man and a woman—who produce children (offspring). They live together and form a social unit under the same name. The children take the name of the family as their own and it becomes part of their identity.

There are other kinds of family structures. Children may grow up without their biological parents. They live with grandparents, or aunts and uncles, or some other relatives who have custody of them. Some children live with adopted parents or legal guardians, perhaps foster parents who are responsible for their care.

Changing Times and Changing Families

Family structure has changed a great deal over the past several decades. At one time, perhaps in the 1930s, intact traditional families were the most common. But society has changed and many families have been fragmented, scattered, or reorganized.

First, there are more working mothers than ever before. In 1972, for example, only twelve million mothers worked outside the home. Since that time, the number has increased 102%. It is estimated that by 1995, two thirds of all preschool-age children and nearly four out of five school-age children will have a mother in the workforce. This means that child care is a big issue in our society and introduces the concept of "an expanded family," where more adults and child-care providers are involved in helping raise children.

Although the number of divorces in our nation is beginning to level off, current projections indicate that 54% of first marriages will end in divorce. Of the 70% who remarry, about half will divorce again. Millions of children are affected. About half of all children will live with a single parent at sometime before their sixteenth birthday and the number is nearly nine out of ten for minority children.

Children being born out of wedlock may soon overtake divorce as the primary cause of families headed by single mothers. Children living with a single parent now account for almost one out of four children (24%), an increase of 5% within the past decade and more than 20% in the past two decades. Sometimes an unexpected death can force a change in a family structure.

The concept of "blended families" is a sign of the times. A man and a woman, with children from previous marriages, may marry. This new unit forces all members to make adjustments and to learn new ways of communicating. Many parents are able to help their children adapt to new family patterns and to learn a new system of relationships. Other parents are unsure of how to help and they ignore the stress and issues that eventually cause serious problems.

Regardless of how families are organized, children learn how to get along with others in order to survive both physically and psychologically. Children learn early in their lives how to read adult behaviors, to know the meaning of certain words and voice tones. As infants, for example, we counted on people around us to care for us and to assume parenting roles. We needed them to provide food, shelter, protection, and to meet our basic needs. In this process, no matter who the parenting adults might be, groundwork was being laid for some of our life-long attitudes, behaviors, and beliefs.

There are many different kinds of family structures where children learn who they are and how to get along in the world. Some families function better than others. Some families are so dysfunctioning and fragmented they create problems for their members.

Functioning and Dysfunctioning Families

Fully-functioning families, regardless of size, provide an atmosphere which facilitates personal growth and humanness. There is a sense of love and caring which fosters trust, mutual respect, and a positive view of life. Parents view themselves as teachers and help their children learn socially acceptable ways of living.

Children who grow up in functioning families are encouraged and feel supported. They are treated with kindness and a gentle firmness as they learn how to accept more responsibilities and independence. They share in family tasks and their contributions are valued. These children tend to grow up with high self-esteem and a sense of personal worth.

Of course, no family is perfect. There are going to be stressful problems which distract members and make them less functioning than at other times. There are going to be conflicts when people have different opinions, interests, and needs. However, these problems and conflicts can be solved, more often than not, through caring and healthy approaches in a fully-functioning family.

In dysfunctioning families problems are resolved with less satisfaction. There is more misunderstanding and hurt, and some members may feel they have been treated unfairly. There may be more punishment, which results in distrust, fear, and resentment. This kind of family does not handle stress very well and as it increases, relationships often break down and more problems result.

When children grow up in a dysfunctioning family, they often develop powerful personal resources, for better or for worse. They devise personal defenses (defense mechanisms) which help them cope with adults who put them through emotional stress. These secret, and most often unconscious defenses, may be temporary, or they may become habits which last a lifetime. Quite often children of these families become dysfunctioning adults, who in turn have dysfunctioning families. It is a self-defeating pattern that needs to be broken.

Children who live in abusive and chaotic families learn to be wary of adults and to distrust them. Abuse of alcohol or drugs, for instance, make parents act in unpredictable ways. Sometimes they are loving and thoughtful, while at other times they may be insensitive and even frightening. Childhood defenses develop when a child experiences the home as an illogical and confusing place to be. These defenses may work well within the home, but they too often lead to personal dysfunctioning in other situations.

Therapists and counselors are trained to work with people who have grown up in troubled families. These professionals have noted that many of their clients rely on childhood defenses that are no longer appropriate. Some have become too intense. Typical disorders or problems that prevent people from dysfunctioning families in realizing their potential include:

- fear of abandonment
- fear of intimacy
- fear of failure
- distrust and self-doubt
- intense mood swings
- depression
- eating disorders
- lying
- casual sex or sexual disorders
- dependence on drugs or alcohol
- violent behaviors
- impulsiveness and lack of control
- inability to relax
- critically judging others and thinking negatively
- constant search for approval by others
- compulsive need to be recognized
- lack of self-respect and self-esteem

Family Systems of Communication

There are many different patterns of family relationships and they each have their own unique system of communication. The patterns and systems are so numerous it would be impossible to identify them all. For our purposes, a few general ones can be mentioned here: authoritarian, permissive, and democratic.

Authoritarian families

In authoritarian families the parenting adults, no matter who they may be, make demands. They set and enforce the rules and children must abide by them or suffer painful consequences. Autocratic parents operate from a power base and value obedience. There is little room, if any, for a discussion of ideas or feelings. Respect and recognition are determined by how well the children follow directions and meet adult expectations.

In one study, two out of five (40%) high school youths said their parents were too strict and too rigid. In such families there tends to be more tension and conflict. There is more hostility, arguments, disrespect, and distance between parents and children. Life at home is an on-going power struggle, with warring camps lined up against each other.

Ironically, surveys of adults about their parenting skills show that most parents are inclined toward the authoritarian or autocratic approach. They believe it is the role of parents and say, "That's the way it was when I was a kid. I never questioned my parents. I did what I was told." Such an approach in these times, however, only seems to create additional problems.

This parenting style might work when children are little but, as they grow older and stronger, authoritarian methods are challenged. Children rebel and try to strike back. There are more conflicts among family members. If the parents lack tolerance or are too punitive, then any kind of healthy rebellion is seen as hopeless and the young may feel helpless.

Permissive families

Some parents, perhaps as a reaction to the parenting styles they experienced as children or because they are too self-centered and involved in their own lives, form permissive families. There are few rules, restraints, or guidelines. All members are on their own, free to find what works best for them.

When a conflict of interest takes place, family members do as they please, often trying to avoid one another. Children and adults are uninvolved, almost indifferent to what is happening in their lives. One teenager said it was like living in a "House of Mannequins." Everyone was polite enough, but nobody seemed to notice. They were like ships passing in the night, hardly noticing what was happening to others. The permissiveness also communicated a lack of caring, support, and love. Frequently, there is a loneliness among family members which breeds self-doubt, a lack of personal worth, and a sense of abandonment.

A third of the parents in one study said they believed their children could do what they wanted, as long as it did not hurt someone else. It was assumed that such a position would help them to become responsible and independent. Some of these same parents also said, "I'm probably too lenient" and "I let my child get away with too many things." "I should probably be tougher, but I'm not sure what to do." Many well-intended permissive parents are uncertain about their parenting roles and skills. They neglect their responsibilities and rely on the hope that everything will work out okay.

Several studies have been completed which tracked more than 100 children for nearly twenty years. These studies concluded that parents who are not harshly punitive, but who set firm boundaries and stick to them, are much more likely to have children who are high achievers and who get along well with others.

Democratic families

In democratic families, parents try to create positive relationships based on mutual respect and encouragement. Everyone's contributions are valued, even though one's wishes may not be granted. Natural and logical consequences replace rewards and punishments, which enable a child to assume some independence and take responsibility.

Democratic parents are open to suggestions and are willing listeners. They are sensitive to feelings and recognize that not everyone's interests and needs can always be met. There are bound to be differences and solving family conflicts are a part of living and growing. Children are treated with fairness and firmness. There is a kind and friendly atmosphere in the house, as family members try to be considerate of each other.

There are a lot of books about parenting. No one is quite sure what works best. The democratic approach appeals to most children. They would like to be heard and have their rights recognized. This approach also appeals to parents, but it is hard work and it takes a lot of cooperative effort.

Most families have found some kind of blend of these approaches, drawing upon their own family background, personal values, education, and beliefs about the role of parents. The circumstances and events in a family, from time to time, can also influence parenting styles.

One father said that he had tried being both an authoritarian and a permissive parent. In both cases the results were disastrous. "At first I was too strict and then when we ran into problems, I gave up and was too easy. That only caused more problems and made matters worse between my wife and me. We argued over what should be done with the kids and who was responsible. It seemed as if it was us against them."

This couple took some parenting courses at a local community college and decided on a compromise—an approach which fell between the kinds mentioned above. They set rules and expected some resistance. They wanted to be flexible, open to negotiation. They tried to avoid being rigid and to use their best judgment when saying "no" or "yes" to requests. They listened more to their children and worked at hearing feelings as well as ideas. They viewed conflicts less as a personal flaw and more as a natural part of a family with different personalities. "I can't begin to tell you how much it meant to all of us when we took time to listen and to use some plain old communication skills.

Sometimes the family patterns of relating and communicating are not always clear. Closeness and personal involvement among family members may depend upon special circumstances, sudden events or problems, types of personalities, family background, and traditions. Such factors can make family members act differently from time to time, especially under stress.

Common Problems Facing Families and Young People

Problems are part of living together and growing up. Some are more serious than others. Some are a result from poor relationships between children and their parents. Others come about between young people and their teachers or friends. Some are brought on by the changing world in which we live.

Young people want to talk about their problems. They have goals and worries. They want an opportunity to explore their thoughts and feelings. It is stimulating and productive to explore alternatives and to think about how to solve problems.

One study of more than 8,000 adolescents showed that young people worried most about school achievement, making friends, personal appearance, substance abuse, parental relationships, and social issues. How do these compare to your own concerns? Are they the same or different from those of your peers? How do these worries affect families?

"I worry a lot about how I'm doing in school," said one fifth grade student. It's important to make good grades." Getting good grades in school can reassure one's self-image and please parents. "It keeps my parents off my back," said one student. When students do not do well in school, they risk being ridiculed and labeled "dumb." The concern of doing well in school usually declines with those high school students who have had little academic success in elementary or middle school. They may still feel some pressure from teachers and parents, but their primary interests turn elsewhere. They often become defensive about their progress in school, perhaps taking an "I don't care" position.

Junior high school girls said one of their greatest worries was physical appearance. They spent a lot of time thinking about what they were going to wear and the latest fads and styles in clothes. They talked about conflicts between them selves and their parents, who disapproved of the way they dressed or who would not buy them the kind of clothes they wanted to wear. One girl was caught shoplifting and said she just wanted to have some clothes like her friends.

Another major concern among young people is "having friends." How do you make new friends? How do you tell your friends that you do not want to do something? What do you do when you lose your best friend? One young man said, "My friends drink too much at parties and I'm not sure I want to go out with them anymore, but they are my friends." How can you help a friend who is in trouble? What do you do if you don't have any friends? In almost every survey, loneliness is cited as one of the most common problems among teenagers.

As people think about themselves and their problems, they sometimes are unaware of the needs and concerns of other family members. They may not be sensitive to fragile relationships. Lack of money or personal satisfaction from a job can make people unhappy and difficult to live with. Some parents, who experience stressful job conditions or employer demands, might unknowingly take out their frustrations on family members. When communication among family members is poor, then stressful situations often get intense and lead to more problems.

Peervention— **What Peers Can Do**

Bridging the Communication Gap was a film developed by Betsy Folk and a group of peer facilitators to help parents and their children learn more about each other. Too often parents and their children drift apart and fail to understand one another, especially during the teenage years. The primary problem is a lack of communication. The film showed peers interviewing parents and students on a variety of topics.

The film, or perhaps a home-made video tape at your school, can be used as a catalyst with a group of parents and their children. It can be used on Parent's Night at the school, where discussion groups are led by peer facilitators who pose such questions as: 1) What are two questions you would really like to ask your child? Parent? 2) What three words would you use to describe the relationship between you and your child? Parent? 3) What is one thing you are most proud of about your child? Parent? 4) What is one issue that needs to be resolved in order to make things better in the family?

A Parent Day, sponsored by the peer leadership class, at the school encourages parents to attend the school and to talk about their experiences. This peer-led discussion group might ask each parent to share "Words of Wisdom They Ignored" and "Words of Wisdom that Should Not Have Been Ignored." They might also talk about people who influenced them the most when they were in high school and how that influence still remains or has changed.

A peer facilitator hotline, which can be directed to parents or to students, could add a positive approach to promoting understanding of parent/child conflicts, special issues, or problems. One school system has established evening family counseling centers in some of the high schools where night classes are offered. Parents, with their children, can meet with peer facilitators and a counselor, who co-lead a family meeting.

Peer facilitators working as big brothers and sisters often model communication and interpersonal skills for other students who may not be living in a positive family atmosphere. For example, a high school student may be a very special friend to an elementary school student who comes from a single parent family. Big brothers and sisters can also meet once a week with their "buddies" to be a playmate and to discuss interests and concerns.

Kenneth is a tenth grader whose parents divorced when he was in the fourth grade. He is now a peer facilitator who co-leads a group of elementary school children with the school's counselor. The "Children of Divorce Group" was organized by the counselor to enable the children to share their common concerns and fears. The group was designed to help the children adjust and to gain the most from school, even though they were still struggling with the changes in their families. This group was voluntary, although parent permission was obtained. It is rare for parents to decline an invitation for their children to be in such a group.

By helping the children, Kenneth also learned about his own fears and some unresolved issues he still carried. He listened and helped facilitate the discussions. While helping the children, he gained some personal insights himself. Peers who help others often help themselves in the process.

Activity 12.1
A Letter to My Children

Purpose:

To increase awareness of parenting styles and parent/child relationships.

Materials:

Paper and pencil

Procedures:

1. Begin by listing items under the following headings:

   My Family—List who is in your family, ages, order of birth, and one characteristic of each.

   How My Family Solves Problems—List two problems and ways in which your family makes decisions or resolves problems.

   Changes I'd Make to Improve My Family—Be specific and creative.

   Things I Have Learned About Parenting From My Family

   What I Promise You as Your Parent—List some things you plan to do as a parent someday.

2. Referring to your list, write a five paragraph letter entitled, "A Letter to My Children," which tells about the kind of parent you would like to be and the promises you want to make. Include some reference to each of the five topics to help form your letter.

3. After your letter is written, read it to someone in your family for a reaction. What do they think you left out? Were there any surprises?

4. Choose someone in the class with whom to share your writing experience and the discussion you had with a family member. How are your experiences similar and different? Facilitate each other's talk about the letter to the child.

Key Questions

What events seemed to shape your opinions and attitudes about family communication patterns? What experiences have led to the advice you are giving yourself about parenting? What events seemed to have influenced your own parents' style of parenting? How do you feel about being a parent someday?

Robert D. Myrick and Betsy E. Folk

Activity 12.2
The Family Line-Up

Purpose:

To increase understanding of one's unique place in the family unit.

Materials:

Paper and pencil

Procedures:

1. Begin by listing on a piece of paper the names, ages, and birth order of your family members, including yourself.

2. Next to each person's name on the list, put three words which might best describe that person's personality.

3. The class is divided into four groups representing 1) Only Child; 2) Middle Child; 3) Youngest Child; and, 4) Oldest Child. Pick the group which describes your birth order and join it.

4. With your group members, discuss the following:

    a. What are the advantages of being in the position in your family?

    b. What are the disadvantages?

    c. What are some of your feelings about being in this birth position?

    d. How are you alike and different from your brothers or sisters? Or, if an only child, then from your parents?

5. Look at the following generalizations about birth order:

    Only Child: You can convince people to agree with you. You get high grades. You're self-centered and relate well with adults.

    Middle Child: You are easy going... the life of the party. You are rarely shy with the opposite sex. You prefer not to compete but to compromise.

    Youngest Child: You get away with a lot. You usually get things your way. You feel less pressure than older siblings. You are treated as "the baby."

    Oldest Child: You are the high achiever in the family. There are more expectations and responsibilities. You keep feelings to yourself and conform more to parent's wishes. You like neatness and organization.

In your same groups, discuss whether or not the characterizations are true for you and members of your family.

Key Questions

In what ways does birth order influence family roles and expectations? Which is more important in terms of influencing personality development, birth order or

Chapter 13

The Prevention of Alcohol and Drug Abuse

The abuse of alcohol and drugs is a terrifying problem threatening our society. Even though other forces, such as nuclear warfare, may be potentially more damaging, nothing has been more destructive to our nation and its potential than the abuse of drugs and alcohol.

When used properly to treat medical problems, prescribed drugs can correct an imbalance in body chemistry, protect against disease, relieve tension and pain, and provide some relief. When used as a mood elevator to create an intoxicating effect, as some kind of misconceived form of recreation, then drugs are dangerous medications, no matter whether they are legal or illegal substances.

The United States has the highest rate of drug abuse of any developed nation on earth. It is obvious that older generations, including many contemporaries, have failed. They have provided poor examples and the large majority have ignored the problem, most hoping that maybe it will simply go away. Denial by parents, school personnel, and students only makes them part of the problem. Sooner or later, the abuse of alcohol and drugs affects everyone, including the nonusers.

More than others, people who use and abuse drugs are responsible for more car accidents, more child abuse, more job absenteeism, more broken marriages and family relationships, and more personal health problems. They detract from the general welfare of others. Their habits and consequences cost taxpayers millions of dollars. Perhaps the real tragedy is that so much human potential is wasted and lost.

The abuse of alcohol and drugs is a complex problem. No one is quite sure how to fight the war against drugs. But, it is becoming clear that the most important battles are fought not in congress, or in governmental agencies. Rather, they are waged in the everyday decisions, values, and actions of young people. It is rare for an adult who has never smoked or indulged in the use of a self-destructive drug to develop such a habit later in life. To the contrary, those who can resist becoming involved are much more likely to be in control and to live healthy lives.

One alarming fact is that experimentation with alcohol and drugs is starting at an earlier age than in the preceding decades. The first experience with marijuana, for example, is at about 11 1/2 years of age and for alcohol it is even younger. Four out of ten sixth graders say there is pressure from other students to use alcohol and about 35% of the fourth graders surveyed said drinking is "a big problem" for their age group.

A national survey of elementary school students found that television and movies are a major source of myths about alcohol and drugs for pre-teenagers. Some of these myths persist through the teenage years and into adulthood. For example:

Myth 1: All famous and talented people drink alcohol and use drugs.

Myth 2: Having a drink or using drugs is the sociable thing to do.

Myth 3: They (drugs and alcohol) are not going to hurt you when you are young, healthy, and know what you are doing.

Myth 4: Drugs and alcohol improve performance.

Myth 5: Drinking is the "best way to party," to have fun and be social.

Because so much publicity and millions of dollars have been poured into the war against drugs, there is an encouraging trend away from using illicit drugs. It is no longer "cool" to do drugs. The possible consequences are so risky that a more educated generation of young people is saying no to drugs and deciding to work for drug-free schools and a drug-free society. People's attitudes are changing.

Robert D. Myrick and Betsy E. Folk

Yet, drugs have become cheaper and are still a part of almost every community. The number of people using the highly addictive form of the drug known as crack has increased as much as 33% within the last five years. The war against drugs has only begun.

In many respects, it will not be the older generations who will lead the battles and win the war. Old habits are hard to break and casual attitudes about alcohol and drug usage have been part of older Americans' thinking for many years. It is the new generations of young people where the best hope lies. This is one of the reasons why peer facilitators are volunteering to work with elementary school students, helping them to learn how to resist pressures and to make healthier choices. In doing so, most peer helpers have increased their own awareness and, subsequently, reaffirmed their decisions to say no to drugs.

In our society a large majority of families have broken down. The family is viewed as the base for which values are formed and behaviors are modeled. Many children lack stable and healthy family environments which could give them support and understanding. Therefore, people are turning to the school as the primary "intact" system for providing support to all students. It is a place where positive peer interactions can make a significant difference. It is where peer facilitators can work to help create a drug-free society.

The Gateway Drugs

Nicotine is an active ingredient found in tobacco. Each year over 390,000 Americans die prematurely from the effects of smoking. Cigarette smokers have a 70% greater chance of early death than non-smokers. The habit causes 85% of all lung cancer deaths, 30 to 40% of heart and blood vessel disease, and 80-90% of pulmonary disease.

On the bright side, more people are making an educated decision not to smoke. About 29% of adults now smoke cigarettes, down from 40% about 25 years ago. Fewer teenagers are smoking, but the nonsmoker rate has stabilized within the past few years, and there are still far too many smokers. The more years of school people have, the less likely they are to smoke. Legislative efforts have resulted in smoking being restricted in many public places. Nonsmokers are beginning to realize the ill effects of being around smokers and inhaling secondary smoke. The Surgeon General's goal is to have a smoke free society by the year 2000.

Alcohol (beer, wine, wine coolers, and liquor) is America's preferred substance to abuse. Alcoholic beverages as an industry grosses over twelve billion dollars in sales each year. In a statistical sense, teenagers drink alcohol as much as adults, with one out of twenty high school seniors drinking every day. With so much attention focused on the "drug problem" as related to marijuana, cocaine, crack, and other drugs, not as much attention has been given to the most serious problem—teenage boozing.

Why do teenagers drink alcohol? Television commercials and magazine advertisements can make drinking look very attractive. The National Federation of Drug-Free Youth, on the other hand, has said the real truth in advertising would be:

- It can make you throw up.
- It can make you pass out.
- It can give you hangover.
- It can make you an addict.
- It can interfere with your reproductive system.
- It can wreck your car.
- It can kill your friends.
- It can make you act like an idiot.

Alcohol is a drug, a depressant, and causes more deaths among teenagers than any other substance. It may energize some people and sedate others. Some claim that it gives them a sense of self-confidence, takes away anxiety, makes them laugh, and helps them feel peaceful. Yet, as people drink more, the initial feelings of euphoria are reversed and depression results.

Most young people first get drunk on beer or wine. It is what they can afford. These beverages are just as intoxicating as liquor or "the hard stuff." In 1987 a *Weekly Reader* survey found that four out of ten sixth graders reported feeling peer pressure to use alcohol. Among teenagers there is a growing concern related to binge drinking, which involves several drinks at a time. It demonstrates a lack of knowledge about alcohol.

Cigarettes and alcohol are considered "gateway drugs" because they pave the way for the use of other drugs and substances. This is where teenagers typically start. While there are exceptions, most people who use hard drugs have progressed through various stages of using the gateway drugs.

The Illegal Drugs

Marijuana (also called pot, grass, weed, reefers, herb, or smoke) was once thought to be a rather harmless mind-altering drug.

It is now known that it is a complex drug, containing 426 chemicals that when smoked convert into 2,000. Today's marijuana joint is much more powerful than the ones smoked during the 1960s when it was a popular drug of choice among young people.

With increased drug testing in work places, those who smoke marijuana may be threatened with a loss of their jobs. First, it takes the body as long as thirty days to rid itself of the THC, the primary ingredient, which accumulates in the body's fatty tissues such as the liver, ovaries, testicles, and, of course, the brain. Habitual use destroys brain cells and harms short term memory. Continued use also leads to lethargy, poor attention span, neglect of personal appearance, and a general lack of anything except the thought of getting high. Habitual users have been described as "burnouts," seeming to be slow, dim-witted, and forgetful. Although it may not cause mental disorders, the drug is likely to heighten existing psychological problems.

Another important fact is that marijuana also diminishes the body's ability to protect itself against illness by reducing the division of disease-repelling white blood cells. A regular smoker is more likely to get sick. There is also some evidence that boys who use marijuana before puberty may have less-than-normal sexual development as a result of lowered testosterone, the principal male hormone. The drug has been shown to disrupt the menstrual cycle in adolescent girls.

Cocaine, also called coke or snow, has been made glamorous by the media within recent years, showing it as a way to chase the blues away and of providing a rush of excitement. However, these effects wear off quickly and a psychological crash occurs. What follows is depression, anxiety, irritability, and a lack of motivation. The solution too often is to get more coke and the abuser is on a roller coaster ride, with each subsequent "downer" becoming more intense and creating a greater craving for the drug. A self-destructive cycle is set in motion. And worse, the horrendous ride continues as there is a false sense of well-being and security, tricking users into thinking that they are in control and cannot overdose.

According to a cocaine hotline study, the average teenager progresses from first use to chronic abuse in just fifteen and a half months, as compared to four years for adults. The drug can quickly becomes an obsession.

In one experiment, monkeys were given choices of food, water, enjoyable activities, and various drugs, including cocaine. All selected cocaine as their first choice, which they continued to inject until they went into convulsions and died. Such extreme cravings were not found with any other substance.

Crack (base, rock, or crank) is a freebase variant made by mixing cocaine crystals with baking soda. A paste is created which, after it hardens, is cut into chips. It is then smoked. The name crack comes from the crackling sound the drug makes when ignited. It has been called the "fast food of drugs" because chips are sold for as little as five dollars, putting it within reach of many young people. There is an intense high, multiplying the effect of cocaine five to ten times. Many people lose control and become violent or suicidal. It may be the most addictive substance known to man and the most destructive.

Darin, a teenager, said, "I started using it just so I could say I had done it. I didn't want the guys to think I was a wimp. Then, everything just went to pieces. I heard about guys dying from it, and all that stuff, but it didn't make no difference. I had to have it. I stopped caring about everything, except getting that hit from the pipe. I would be out of school for a week straight, just doin' what I could to get money to get my stuff. I broke into houses, stole from my parents and girl friend, and.... It was hell, man. And you know, that wasn't really like me. I can't blame my parents, as they are okay. But, something just happened. If I hadn't got some treatment (hospital) I'd probably be dead or in jail right now."

A research study released in 1990 by the National Institute on Drug Abuse showed that more than a quarter of a million American teenagers (262,000), most of them boys, have used potentially harmful performance-enhancing anabolic steroids. This number may be conservative because it did not take into account school dropouts or those who would not admit to usage. The number seems to be increasing, especially since steroids have been linked to world-class athletes who use them to increase muscle mass and strength. In addition, parents, coaches, and others indirectly encourage the use of such drugs by putting pressure on young people to compete and win. More than half of the users surveyed (55%) believed that their parents probably knew that they used steroids.

At a time when most teenagers are struggling to accept their bodies and are worried about their appearances, these secret drugs can be appealing. Steroids are viewed as a short cut or a quick fix in an attempt to gain strength. Yet, there are many health problems related to steroid use, including: sterility, increased cholesterol levels, high blood pressure, liver damage, increased irritability, and even violent behavior. An educational campaign needs to be aimed especially at young athletes.

Peervention—
What Peers Can Do

On many school campuses across the United States, there are Students Against Drunk Driving (SADD) chapters. Peer facilitators can assist these chapters in their projects, such as organizing programs and presenting information. One group of about fifteen high school seniors, for example, dressed themselves in all black clothes and painted their faces white. They wanted to emphasize that if people drink alcohol before going to a school dance, then they might not be alive to come to school the next week.

One classmate said, "I laughed about it, at first, then it seemed kind of eerie, especially when they wouldn't speak with anyone. One time I looked at Jon and started thinking how sad it would be if he were not part of our class anymore." The next day students talked in small groups about what they could do to prevent alcohol from ruining their school dances.

Project Graduation is an organized effort by students and adults in one community to offer a drug-free alternative to "getting drunk" on graduation night. Designed to provide a safe environment, it gives seniors and their guests, a chance to laugh, dance, and party in an atmosphere free of drugs and alcohol. The community sponsors an all night (10:00 P.M. until 4:30 A.M.) "celebration" at a gymnasium for the graduating classes in the area. It features a band and music. Activities, coordinated by the students, can include volleyball, casino and arcade games, and limbo contests. Food is served from a teenager's dream menu.

Prizes, which increase in value throughout the night, help keep everyone at the party and off the streets. It is an evening full of excitement to provide memories for a lifetime.

DARE is a sixteen-week prevention education program for kindergarten through eighth grade. Its focus is on drug education and the instructors are often uniformed police officers. It *dares* students to say "no" to drugs and tries to build their self-esteem. Peer facilitators can assist group leaders in such educational programs.

Some peer facilitators have been key leaders in helping form "Just Say No" clubs. There are now over 15,000 nationally affiliated clubs. They meet in schools, churches and synagogues, and in community centers and agencies. Saying "no" during adolescence has shown to be a critical factor for being able to resist drugs later in life.

You and your friends might want to put together a multi media presentation which is related to your school and community. You can sponsor projects which feature learning activities, bulletin boards, and posters. Video taped productions might also encourage students to take a stand against alcohol and drugs.

Reach America is an intensive anti-drug program in Arizona which is taught by teenagers who attend a two-day training seminar. They learn about drugs' effects and how to present information through skits and discussion groups. They must pass a test at the end of the seminar before they can participate in the program's presentations.

"My Choice... Drug Free" was the message a group of high school students wanted to send throughout the school, businesses, and the community during Red Ribbon Week. They worked with their local Council on Alcohol and Drug Abuse as part of a nationwide campaign in October. The group made banners, stickers, buttons, and helped distribute them. In addition to the poster and door-decorating contests, groups of students made up video taped skits with drug-free messages which were judged and prizes were awarded. The campaign put more pressure on students who use drugs and "validated" those who do not.

It is never too early to learn about the ill effects of alcohol and drug abuse. High school students can go to elementary and middle schools as part of a drug-free school program. They might lead students through learning activities which focus on awareness, knowledge, attitudes, and peer pressures. Students want to talk about their ideas and concerns, what they see and hear, and about alternatives.

Learning is more than hearing a lecture on substance abuse. It is more than talk about long term risks, which generally have little meaning to young students who believe they are invulnerable and who think they have a long life ahead of themselves. It is more than telling horror stories and trying to create unpleasant images of what happens to people who abuse drugs and alcohol. Rather, it is a complete educational process where students explore causes, effects, alternatives, goals, values, and lifestyles.

You may be able to help your classmates by being aware of the stages of behavioral change which suggest that a person is having problems with alcohol or drugs. You may need to use the problem solving model or confrontation to bring matters to a head, but your timely assistance may also save a life.

It has been estimated that thirty million American children live in alcoholic families. Many of these children will become addicted too, as they continue a family tradition. They will become tomorrow's alcoholics unless they have an opportunity to talk about their situations, examine the values that they want to live by, and to be supported in their efforts to break the family pattern. Support groups, both in and out of school, can be co-led by peer facilitators.

In Alateen groups for young people whose lives have been affected by someone else's drinking, several questions are asked and discussed openly. Among these are:

- Do you have a parent, close friend, or relative whose drinking upsets you?

- Do you cover up your real feelings by pretending you do not care?

- Do you tell lies to cover up for someone else's drinking problem?
- Do you make threats such as, "If you don't stop drinking, I'll...."
- Do you feel that you are part of the problem?
- Do you believe that no one could possibly understand the way you feel?
- Have you ever considered calling the police because of the drinker?
- Do you ever treat people (teachers, classmates, teammates, and so forth) unjustly because you are angry at someone who is drinking too much?

Although most schools have some kind of anti-drug and anti-alcohol program, one study of teenagers estimated that nearly two thirds of high school seniors use alcohol, 29% smoke cigarettes, and 18% use marijuana. One of two high school students will try an illicit drug before graduation, according to the National Institute on Drug Abuse. Part of the problem is the social acceptability of drinking, with only 27% of high school seniors believing that alcohol is harmful. Until this changes, further gains in the reduction of alcohol and drug abuse is unlikely.

Activity 13.1
Face the Experts

Purpose: To provide an opportunity for students to examine issues related to the prevention of alcohol and drug abuse.

Materials: None

Procedures:

1. The class will be divided into four groups. Each group will take a turn being a panel of "experts" on alcohol and drug abuse.

2. The panel of experts sits in front of the room, facing the others. The other three groups, acting as news reporters, take turns asking questions of the experts. Each group takes a few minutes to develop questions for the panel.

3. After the panel of experts has answered six questions, two from each of the three groups of "reporters," all the groups rotate. Each group eventually serves as experts.

4. The following questions might be posed to the different panels?
   a. Why do you think the United States has the highest rate of drug abuse in the world?
   b. Why is child abuse related to alcohol and drug abuse?
   c. Why cannot people simply stop drinking or using drugs when they want to?
   d. Why does experimentation of drugs start at so early an age?
   e. Should we have anti-smoking laws? If so, what kind? If not, why not?
   f. What should society do about mothers who take drugs while they are pregnant?
   g. Should children turn their parents into legal authorities if the parents use illegal drugs?
   h. To what extent is teenage boozing a problem? In our community?
   i. Should students who participate in school activities take random drug tests at school?
   j. Should school authorities be able to search student lockers in search of illegal drugs?
   k. Do warnings about alcohol and drug abuse really make a difference with teenagers?
   l. What recommendations do you have for prevention of alcohol and drug abuse?

Key Questions

What other questions can be asked? What information was missing in order to answer the questions effectively? How many of the answers were based on opinions? Facts? Do peer facilitators need to be experts on drug abuse in order to help others?

Robert D. Myrick and Betsy E. Folk

Activity 13.2
The Alcohol and Drug Abuse Survey

Purpose: To discover the extent to which alcohol (or other drugs) are used and abused by students.

Materials: Survey form

Procedures:

1. Take the "Alcohol and Drug Abuse Survey."

2. Next, help make copies of the survey to distribute to other students in your school.

3. With your classmates, decide where you can best administer the survey (e.g. in classes, the cafeteria, the hallways or other appropriate places). Decide also on when and where a sample of the student population can best be obtained (e.g. all English classes).

4. Administer the survey, perhaps with another peer, being sure to emphasize that student names will not be used and that it is important that respondents be candid and truthful.

5. After the survey forms have been collected, the class can tally the results.

6. As a class examine and discuss the results.

7. Then, decide on how the results can be used to help develop a peer facilitator project, with specific kinds of interventions.

8. Share the final results with students, faculty, and administrators.

Key Questions

How accurate do you think the results are? Does the sample reflect accurately the total school? As you look at the results to each of the items, were there any surprises? Do you know of anyone who would benefit from the help of a peer facilitator project aimed at the prevention of alcohol and drug abuse? Were there other items which could have been added to the survey?

The Alcohol and Drug Abuse Survey

Grade_____ Male or Female _____

Directions: Circle the appropriate response for each item (Y = Yes; N = No; and NA = Not Applicable). Do not sign your name.

1. Have you ever drunk an alcoholic beverage?   Y   N   NA

2. Have you ever been a passenger in a car with a driver who has been drinking alcohol?   Y   N   NA

3. Have you ever been to a party where kids drink alcoholic beverages?   Y   N   NA

4. Have you drunk an alcoholic beverage more than on three occasions in your life?   Y   N   NA

5. Do you sometimes drink alcohol because it makes you feel more at ease with others?   Y   N   NA

6. Do you get drunk or "loaded" at least once a month?   Y   N   NA

7. Have you drunk alcohol within the last week?   Y   N   NA

8. Do you sometimes drink alcohol because it helps you forget your worries?   Y   N   NA

9. Do you sometimes drink alcohol even when you don't want to?   Y   N   NA

10. Do you go to parties mainly to drink alcohol?   Y   N   NA

11. Do you usually get mad or angry when you drink?   Y   N   NA

12. Has anyone ever tried to stop you from drinking alcohol?   Y   N   NA

13. Have you ever encouraged someone else to drink alcohol?   Y   N   NA

14. Do you think alcohol abuse is a problem for you?   Y   N   NA

15. Do you think that your friends will understand and accept you if you say no to alcohol?   Y   N   NA

16. Do you feel peer pressure to drink alcohol?   Y   N   NA

17. Is drinking alcohol a bigger problem than using drugs?   Y   N   NA

18. Did you experiment with alcohol in middle school?   Y   N   NA

19. Did you experiment with alcohol in elementary school?   Y   N   NA

20. Would you talk to a peer helper if you were having a problem with drinking alcohol?   Y   N   NA

Robert D. Myrick and Betsy E. Folk

Chapter 14

The Prevention of Body Assault

We live in a violent world, where physical force is used to injure people. Daily, you are likely to read about in any newspaper or see on any television news report a crime in which someone was physically assaulted.

The majority of adolescents and adults have grown up seeing and hearing about violence and physical abuse, if not personally then on television or in the movies. We are used to hearing about crimes and how the weak and defenseless are abused.

We shake our heads in disbelief and are silently thankful it was not us.

Violence is woven into the fabric of American society to such an extent that there are victims in every community.

It may be hard to visualize our nation as young, but it is. In our 200-year-old history, there have been many changes. Many of us still remember seeing the old "gun slinger" Western movies, where the law of the land was often settled by who was the strongest, toughest, and meanest. Primitive thinking still believes that people are best controlled by the threat of violence. For instance, if you murder someone you should be put to death. Or, if you hit someone you should be spanked or paddled.

This same mentality, regrettably, has too often been a part of parenting. Many fathers and mothers, out of frustration and anger, have used extreme roughness to discipline their children. There are parents who are so unhappy with themselves and so full of hostility that they lash out at their children, as if they were defenseless objects. Psychologists have tried to account for explosive and callous behavior, citing family history, lack of parent training and skills, personality changes as a result of drugs or alcohol, and a displacement of the parents' own frustration and pain on children who cannot fight back. Regardless of the reason, personal safety and personal rights of children should not be violated.

Some school authorities still want to paddle or rely on "corporal punishment" when students break school rules. This approach to discipline is beginning to disappear in many states. It is temporarily effective in most cases.

Because physical punishment has been accepted for many years as a way to change people's behaviors, many people in society are confused about the use of violence against others. They know it is wrong to use extreme roughness and hope that it would be used only when nothing else has worked.

Some say physical punishment should be used with "hardened" law breakers. Ironically, eight out of ten criminals in prison were hit and abused when they were children. And, what they learned was: "Get them before they get you." "Only the toughest of the tough really make it." "You gotta be mean, or someone is going to do you in."

In some communities, older boys and girls threaten to "beat up" younger students unless they give them money or other favors. It is called extortion. There is always the additional threat of more beatings. "If you tell anyone you will really get it."

Physical assault can be used in a calculated way. It can be a deliberate scheme to try to gain advantage by mistreating others. Some young people have grown up in families or communities where physical assault is considered a way of life.

Physical Abuse

In the United States there are over 1,000,000 cases of child abuse each year ,and over 2,000 children die from the abuse. Physical abuse against children has been increasing over the past few decades. At least the number of reported cases has been growing, especially with little children (less than three years of age). These children suffer both physical and psychological pain. The latter may be the most devastating and long lasting.

The physical damage is usually more obvious—black and blue bruises, unsightly scars, swollen welts, and teary eyes. In some cases there may be burns, absence of hair in patches on the scalp, chipped teeth, or other evidence of trauma. The mental pain may be less visible, sometimes repressed. "This can't be happening to me." "Am I such a bad person that I deserve this?" "What kind of person am I that I should be treated this way?" Wrong conclusions frequently lead to excessive guilt, anxiety, depression, and despair. There is a lowering of self-esteem as the abuse continues.

Sometimes the psychological-self rebels and, feeling helpless, looks for ways to escape. Some victims of physical abuse, in turn, become violent and abusive themselves. They hurt others or they hurt themselves. Destroying property, using profane language, calling names to insult others, and physical fighting are attempts to strike out. Confused emotional thoughts can also lead to striking back in self-destructive ways, including suicidal tendencies. Some victims withdraw from others and seek seclusion, hoping to avoid further beatings.

Some other signs of physical abuse have included extreme dependency, poor peer relationships, lack of ambition, and adjustment problems in school. Many children who have been abused have grown up with the same personality patterns as the abusers: aggressiveness, isolation, and lack of empathy or caring for others. The abused often believe that they have little control over their lives, have little self-confidence, and have little or no hope for the future. Ironically, it is estimated that among abusing parents, as many as 60% were themselves abused as children. This destructive pattern is passed from one generation to another.

Sexual Abuse

According to researchers, approximately one out of ten boys and four out of ten girls will be sexually assaulted. Even if conservative figures were used, with only 2% of the boys and 10% of the girls, it would mean there are over 200,000 new cases of sexual abuse each year.

Most sex offenders are men. Men abuse about 95% of the female victims and 85% of the male victims. The most common age for abuse is eight through twelve years of age. Most female abuse occurs within a family network, whereas boys are more likely to be abused outside the family.

Much of what we know about sexual abuse has come from the survivors, many of whom kept their "dark and dirty secrets" hidden for years and who were afraid that nobody would ever understand or care about them if their stories were told. Through counseling and therapy, victims are able to explore the impact that sexual abuse has had on their lives.

In little children, sexual exploitation creates a premature development of sexual experiences and knowledge. Because it is inappropriate for their age, there is confusion and the development of their personal identity is thwarted. They learn to flirt, talk about sexual matters, or make physical advances before it is age-appropriate. Confusion about social roles and personal identify can lead to social rejection and delinquent behaviors.

Sexually transmitted diseases, early pregnancies, and a self-sacrificing attitude may result when older children are involved. Because sexual abuse is a form of physical abuse, victims often display many of the same symptoms as mentioned above.

State laws make it mandatory for school personnel and health care professionals to report cases of suspected child abuse. This has resulted in a substantial increase in the number of reports being made to child protective agencies. These agencies are overwhelmed and do the best they can to respond, but they need the help of people in the community, including classmates and friends of the abused children. Unfortunately, many cases go unreported.

Even though the laws may have caused some uncomfortable moments for people when they make their reports, many children have received timely and valuable assistance. If a teacher or counselor, for example, suspects that a child is being physically or sexually abused, there is no choice. The case must be reported to appropriate health officials. The good news is that eight out of ten abusive families can be treated with satisfactory results.

More Abuse

The most common type of child abuse is neglect. It happens when parents fail to provide a safe place for their children to live, play, and grow up.

There are a lot of parents to whom parenting does not come naturally. It is not something which magically happens when children are born. To the contrary, many parents are ignorant of their children's needs and how to care for them. Becoming a parent is still something an amateur can do without any required training.

When parents are not prepared, they may unknowingly neglect their children. They might be left alone when they are too young to care for themselves. They may be unsupervised or be allowed to play in unsafe areas. They may find it easy to get to unlocked weapons or poisons like bleach, cleansers, bug sprays, medicines, or gasoline.

In some cases of neglect, children have been left unattended in cars or at home. They may not have adequate clothes or food. A quiet and secure place to sleep may be missing. When they are ill, the parents may ignore or not recognize the symptoms until someone has stepped in to take control. Children born to teenage mothers are more subject to neglect.

Emotional abuse is also common in our society. This happens when unstable parents vent their own frustrations needlessly on their children. They may yell at them, calling them ugly names or telling them how useless they are. The parents may not even realize the damage they are doing when they shout, "You are so stupid. You never get anything right! I wish you had never been born!" Words can hurt, sometimes more than a physical blow. Emotional abuse is an assault on the minds of children which tears at their self-concepts.

Both the abusers and the abused usually have trouble talking with others. They often lack friends and choose to be alone. They can benefit from professional help.

Peervention— ## What Peers Can Do

As a peer facilitator, you may work with some children who may intentionally tell you about their being abused. What will you do? This situation and the general procedures you might follow can be discussed with your peer trainer/coordinator or one of the school counselors. However, in general, you will:

1. Believe what the child has told you. Even if the child has made up the story, which is very rare, help is needed anyway;

2. Tell the child you are sorry about what happened and that you are glad he or she could tell you;

3. Be aware of your own feelings, so as not to judge the person or say something which makes the child feel rejected, embarrassed, or at fault. Fear and anger are common reactions. Stay calm;

4. Tell the child that he or she should go to and talk with the school counselor (or some other responsible adult in the school) and that you will go, too, if the child wants you there.

5. Make no promises or guarantees that are beyond your control and do not promise to keep it a secret.

The basic listening skills and the feedback model that you have learned will be useful to you in times like these. Your primary task is to see that the child gets help through an appropriate referral.

School-based prevention programs are designed to help educate children and adults about child abuse. Nobody is quite sure how much information young children need or what skills they should be taught, but almost everyone believes that something should be done.

Peer facilitators can be involved in programs which focus on personal safety. They might assist teachers and counselors as they present programs which feature a standardized curriculum, videotapes, and filmstrips. In one "safe child" program, a video tape was used to teach children basic concepts about safety, personal rights, assertiveness, and how to seek help if they were being abused. Through role-playing activities, children learned resistance skills and how to confront an abuser. The dramatizations were staged by high school peer facilitators and presented in the elementary schools of a school district.

How can a child stop unwanted touch? How can children stand up to the emotional pressure which perpetrators put on them to keep the abuse a secret? What can they do when they have been forced or bribed to do things against their will? Some researchers now believe that teaching concepts and ideas about abuse and personal safety is not enough; rather, there

Robert D. Myrick and Betsy E. Folk

must be some active skill training and practice. Peer facilitators can help children learn and practice the necessary skills.

Interviews with sex offenders have provided some clues as to how many of them win the confidence of children. "I would try different kinds of contact, such as touching and rubbing the child's back, head, or arm.... And, kept testing the child to see how much she would take before she pulled away...."

Helping children to say no and move away, or to report unwanted touches when a person persists, is valuable. They need to know that "tattling" is a good thing to do when something makes them uncomfortable and they do not know what to do.

In one school district, high school peer facilitators, play-acting as dolls abused by their owners, told classes of elementary school students that promises to keep abuse secret should be broken. They present a play entitled "Secrets in the Toy Room," which is about two magic dolls (Randy and Mandy) who secretly come to life in front of other toys. As toys they are abused by their child owners and they learn that other toys in the room have been abused too. But, everyone is trying to keep it a secret. In the play, the dolls eventually tell their toy maker, a responsible adult, about what is happening to them.

In another high school, peer facilitators developed a puppet show to inform children about child abuse and neglect. They go to first grade classes in all of the eighteen elementary schools in the district. The show, followed by small group discussions led by the peer facilitators, teaches children how to protect themselves and addresses the following issues:

1. Is there a grown up in the school that you can talk to if you have a problem?

2. When someone asks you to keep a secret, should you always do it, no matter what the secret might be?

3. Is being punished and being abused the same thing?

4. Is it okay to leave a little child at home alone?

5. Do grown ups only believe other grown ups?

6. Can a child say "no" to a grown up?

A study took place in two of the schools. One group of children (80) did not see the show or work with the peer facilitators while another group (80) did. An evaluation related to the items above showed a significant and positive difference favoring the prevention program. In addition, 90% of the children who went to the program said that "other kids my age should see the show" and 95% reported "I learned more about the problems children my age can have."

Activity 14.1
Bullies and Victims

Purpose:

To increase understanding of the feelings and behaviors of people who bully or assault others and those who are victimized.

Materials:

None

Procedures:

1. The class will be divided into three groups: Bullies; Victims; and, Helpers. Join one of the groups.

2. The class seating is arranged in two concentric circles, one in the middle and one on the outside (fishbowl).

3. The Bullies begin the activity by sitting in the middle and telling 1) Times when they personally bullied someone else; or, 2) Times when they observed someone bullying others. They try to share their feelings and behaviors from the Bully's viewpoint.

4. The Helper Group, sitting on the outside, then take their turn in the middle of the circle. They share their observations of 1) Feelings experienced by the Bullies; and, 2) Related behaviors to the feelings.

5. Next, the Victims Group takes its turn in the middle and tells 1) Times when they were bullied; or, 2) Times when they saw someone being victimized by a bully. They share the victims viewpoint.

6. Then, the Helpers Group again sits in the middle and members tell what they observed about feelings and related behaviors of the victims. No advice, interpretations, or putdowns are given.

7. Finally, the total group, sitting in one large circle, talks about the activity and their experiences. Special attention is given again to the feelings and behaviors related to being a bully and being victimized.

Robert D. Myrick and Betsy E. Folk

Key Questions

How are the experiences (feelings and behaviors) from the activity related to the topics associated with bodily assault which have been studied in this chapter? Did the activity help you gain any special insights? What help can be given to victims of abuse? What kind of help might be given those who victimize others?

Activity 14.2
Putdowns—Verbal Abuse

Purpose:

To increase understanding of the dynamics associated with verbal abuse.

Materials:

Paper and pencil

Procedures:

1. Make a list of statements that you remember hearing people say in your school or community which were attempts to put other people down. What words were used? Put quotation marks around the phrases. It is not necessary to identify the speaker.

2. Over the next 24 hours, record all the "put down" statements you hear, either directed toward you or others. These may come from television shows or real life situations.

3. Bring your list to class.

4. In a class go around, compile a list of the different putdowns. One person begins by reading, with the appropriate expression, two items from the list. A second person then does the same, without repeating previous statements. Then, a third person follows the same procedure, and so on.

5. If time permits, tally those that were used most often.

6. Discuss the results of this activity in terms of what you saw and heard.

Key Questions

Did you hear more or less putdowns than you expected? What seemed to be the purpose of the putdowns? Did they accomplish their purpose? How did people react when they received a putdown?

Is verbal abuse a prelude to physical abuse? How? Are some putdowns more serious than others? Is teasing different from assault? How? Is there an effective way to deal with those who tease? With those who bully?

Robert D. Myrick and Betsy E. Folk

Chapter 15

The Prevention of Sex-Related Problems

As human beings we all have a need to be loved and touched throughout our lives. About the age of twelve, or earlier, we become aware of our sexual beings. Some people mature earlier than others, but eventually everyone experiences body changes which heightens sexual aware- ness. It is a part of nature. It is a natural process and it is nothing of which to be ashamed or especially proud. It is simply a part of personal development.

As nature prepares people for close and intimate relationships, there is a desire to express affection. There are personal feelings of wanting to be physically close, to give and receive love, and to experience deeper emotions of intimacy.

This can be a time of confusion and uncertainty. Moods and emotions might cause you, for example, to feel very special at one moment and then desperate and undesirable at another. Depending on your peer relationships, you can feel self-confident or you can be full of self-doubt. If you are wise, you will also recognize that nature may prepare you for some experiences before you are intellectually and personally ready to have them.

Sexual maturity brings out the need for "attachments." Boy and girl friendships might develop into closer ties where fondness and loyalty link people together. When a girl says, "He is my boyfriend," it usually implies a deeper commitment to a relationship than "He is a boy who is my close friend." The first suggests a bond that goes beyond a routine friendship.

Every generation of teenagers is confronted with many of the same issues, especially when it concerns the development of one's sexuality. Some questions come earlier than others. Some are answered at one stage, only to have the same or related questions follow later:

"I wonder if she/he likes me?"

"Should I ask her/him to go out with me?"

"Should I let him/her hold my hand?"

"I wonder what the first kiss will be like?"

"What does he/she expect of me?"

"Is it wrong to have these feelings?"

"How can I say no, without losing him/her?"

"Why do I feel like I have to prove myself?"

The responses to these and other questions must be answered by each individual and are based on what you believe and value, as well as accepted information about human growth and development. It is generally recognized that people from diverse backgrounds, cultures, and families can still share many of the same simple beliefs. Among these are: 1) the family is the primary source for values and sex education; 2) schools have the right and responsibility to help parents educate their children about the role that sexuality has in our society and the problems related to it; and, 3) knowledge and reliable information about sexuality and related problems can contribute to responsible decision making.

Studies have shown that a great deal of our information about sexuality is learned through peers. It may take the form of private conversations with a friend or perhaps through a teacher-led classroom discussion. It may take place in a church youth group. Information may also come from books and magazines, musical lyrics, movies and television, or it may come through the "grapevine." These same studies also suggest that far too many teenagers have a lot of misinformation, misunderstanding, and misguided plans.

For instance, sensitive topics include abortion, homosexuality, sexually transmitted diseases, unwanted pregnancies, school-age parents, rape and sexual assaults, and taking responsibility for intimate relationships.

Most sex related issues are controversial. They can be strongly addressed by advocates from either side. Some people are unsure if adolescents, despite what is known about their undeniable development and interests, should talk about sexuality. Yet, in today's world, students need an opportunity to discuss concerns which affect all of society and the future in which they will live.

Teen Pregnancy

There are over 29 million young people between the ages of thirteen and nineteen. You are most likely a member of this group. Approximately twelve million of your age group have had sexual intercourse. For many it was not necessarily a pleasant experience, simply something that happened because emotions flooded logic and the consequences were not considered. For some, the experience was a natural and spontaneous consequence of being progressively more intimate. For others it was something they thought was expected of them or something they wanted to do because it would prove that someone found them physically desirable. For still others, the experience may have been forced on them and they have only regretful memories.

Regardless of the reason for sexual intercourse, numerous studies during the past decade indicate that there has been a significant increase in both pregnancy and the rearing of offspring by single, school-age mothers. There are ten million women in the United States between the ages of 15 and 19, and each year, over 1.1 million of these young women become pregnant. Most sexually active teenagers do not want to become pregnant and almost all the pregnancies are not anticipated.

In comparison, the percentage of teenage pregnancies and child births is significantly higher in the United States than in any other industrialized nation. This trend is a national concern and threatens the well-being of many children, including the children who are having children.

Of all the children born out of wedlock, at least 60% end up on welfare. They are frequently doomed to poverty and eventually become the responsibilities of taxpayers. Although a few rise above the conditions into which they are born, the majority are limited in terms of educational and economic opportunities.

Pregnancy is the most prevalent reason for female students to drop out of school. About 80% who become mothers by age seventeen drop out and never complete high school. More than 90% who are age fifteen and younger do not finish high school and about half of these do not complete the eighth grade. School-age fathers are less likely to drop out of school than school-age mothers, but still the dropout rate is about four out of ten.

Being a young parent is not an easy job. Mental depression can and often does affect teenage parents. In addition, any hopes and dreams of a long term relationship are often shattered. Pregnancy is a major factor in terminating relationships, as more than 85% of all boys who impregnate teenage girls will eventually abandon them. This can lead to the pregnant girl feeling that she has been used and can result in an emotionally painful truth. Teenage mothers are seven times more likely to attempt suicide than female adolescents who are not parents.

What can be done to help reduce the incidence of teenage pregnancies? Sex education can help, but alone it does not seem to be enough. Unfortunately, it seems that too many teenagers seek information about how to prevent pregnancies only months after they have become sexually involved and many fail to follow accepted procedures of birth control.

Fear of loneliness and the strong adolescent sex drive make it difficult to resist the temptation to use another person sexually. One of the biggest problems facing young people is that of loneliness and the efforts to escape it often leads girls and boys to become sexually involved. Sexual exploitation almost always leads to unhappiness.

Sexually Transmitted Diseases (STD)

A sexually transmitted disease (STD) is passed from one person to the next through sexual intercourse. In the past these were known as venereal diseases. Not all such diseases are serious or life threatening, but all should receive prompt medical attention, including chlamydia, herpes, and venereal warts.

Gonorrhea is the most widespread of STD. It can infect the reproductive organs and sometimes cause sterility. Most recently, research has shown that certain strains of the disease are becoming more resistant to medical treatment.

Syphilis is more serious and might develop slowly for months before producing severe pain, heart problems, and possible blindness. It can be dangerous to the fetus of a pregnant women who has contracted the disease.

Approximately six out of ten persons with gonorrhea or syphilis in 1990 were less than 25 years old. It is frightening to know that one out of four persons with such diseases were between 10 and 19 years of age. These are not just diseases for promiscuous adults. They are affecting many young people throughout the nation.

Acquired Immunodeficiency Syndrome (AIDS) is a fatal viral disease. It is transmitted through the exchange of body fluids found in blood, semen, and vaginal secretions. In 1981, doctors diagnosed only 266 people in the United States with AIDS. In 1987 there were about 42,000 cases. In 1991 the number who develop AIDS swells to 270,000.

About 89% of persons known to have AIDS are homosexuals or drug abusers. At one point, it was assumed that only 4% of those with AIDS had become affected through heterosexual contact, but this number has been increasing each year. Infants and children, have been infected through blood transfusions before there was a testing for the AIDS antibody in 1985.

AIDS reduces the body's ability to protect itself against disease. The primary symptoms are high fever, night sweats, weight loss, diarrhea, fatigue, swollen glands, skin rashes, memory loss, and loss of coordination. Those infected with the disease have developed symptoms as early as four months after contact and as late as eight years after becoming infected. Many patients die within two years after the appearance of the disease.

There is no known cure for AIDS. Nobody has ever recovered. There is no known reliable and effective vaccine to prevent people from being infected. Many teenagers apparently do not know the basic facts about AIDS. In a study of San Francisco adolescents, 30% believed there was a cure for the disease and 29% were not aware that it was a STD.

One expert on the subject has predicted that AIDS will become the number one killer of youth, exceeding the number of deaths resulting from automobile accidents. Part of the reasoning for this claim is that so many adolescents are sexually active and irresponsible. They lack concern or deny the existence of the part they play in the epidemic, preferring to think, "It couldn't happen to me." In addition, individuals infected with the AIDS virus may be without symptoms and at the same time be carriers.

To date, there is no evidence that the virus can be spread to others by someone who has AIDS through day to day social or family contact. For this reason, in many school districts, children with the AIDS virus are allowed to attend school.

AIDS is not someone else's problem. As the epidemic spreads, almost all of us will know of someone who has been affected in some way by an AIDS victim. We can all learn to be more compassionate, but it is vitally important to learn more about the nature of the disease and what precautions can be taken to prevent it.

Date Rape

Sexual intercourse is supposed to be a loving experience, one in which the partners feel tenderness and respect for each other. Warm, caring, and sensitive feelings are present. However, not all sexual experiences are positive.

There has been an increasing number of reports about date rape or acquaintance rape. Some teenage girls, for example, have tearfully told counselors of situations where they were intoxicated on a date and then forced to have sex.

They became victims. A person's body is private and all persons have a right to that privacy. Nobody should be forced into an unwanted sexual experience.

Rape is never a loving experience. It is an act of violence. It involves sexual battery and is a statutory offense that is punishable by law in every state. The myth that rape occurs only when a stranger jumps out of the bushes and violently assaults an unsuspecting female is far too prevalent. Many rapes are committed by men who appear to be "regular guys" whom the victims know. The relationship begins with hope and trust only to end in a humiliating and degrading experience where the woman is left feeling hurt, guilty, and helpless.

It is still a mystery why so many men feel it is their right to brutalize women. It may have its origin in unwritten cultural histories or inappropriate remarks which disparage the image of women. Some men and women are taught to use sex as a weapon, as a vengeful means of trying to control or dominate another person. Regardless, date rape is a form of sexual violence which leads to psychological trauma and legal difficulties.

As young people have more opportunity to openly and honestly talk about issues and problems related to sexuality, more personal regard for the rights of others will take place. Respect for an individual's wishes and choices will also grow. Close personal relationships will be stronger, healthier, and more meaningful. Society will benefit.

Peervention— **What Peers Can Do**

Sexuality, and related problems, is a major issue which needs to be addressed in early developmental years. Some inappropriate attitudes are formed in elementary school. One group of high school peer facilitators co-led a series of human growth and development programs with school counselors and teachers. Their presence implied that "students" can talk about sexual topics and need not be embarrassed or ashamed.

Many middle school students are beginning puberty. They have many questions and already face dilemmas. Unfortunately, society's casual attitude is often communicated to vulnerable young teenagers. The mystery of sexuality too often turns to horror stories for those whose bodies are changing. Middle school is a time when many students are pressured into "just going along" with whatever is happening. It is difficult to take a stand against someone or something when being popular is the primary concern. Boys and girls make jokes about sex, failing to realize that the jokes often imply myths and inappropriate stereotypes which distort the reality of sexual experiences.

A 14-year-old may want to talk with someone about the pressures to be reckless and the desire to get involved in sexual activities. Besides being a good listener, a peer facilitator can help the student to think through some of the consequences and the factors which seem to be influencing decisions. At one point, it might be appropriate to refer the student to a school counselor.

Some girls do not know or refuse to acknowledge that they are pregnant. A 17-year-old girl gave birth to a baby in a high school bathroom stall. She had gone to the school's health clinic complaining of a stomach pain and later told paramedics after giving birth that she did not know she was pregnant. "I know it sounds impossible," said the school's social worker, "but some girls want so badly to believe it's not true. It's like they can wish it away, or like it didn't happen." One counselor said that she encounters at least six pregnant girls a year who deny their condition until it is brought to their attention by another student or teacher who notices.

One group of peer facilitators designed a presentation on date rape. They presented their program to other students, encouraging them to think about the related issues. They hoped to increase student awareness of the problem and discourage boys and girls from playing games resulting in violent acts. Honest exchanges attack myths such as "When she says No, she really means Yes." "You are not a real man unless you can get her to have sex with you."

Peer facilitators can also lead group discussions which help promote the concept of gender-equity. Gender-equity implies that females have as many rights as males. The interests and welfare of both genders must be respected.

In most schools efforts are made to help students think about development and sex related problems. Sometimes there are special programs where public health officials present information and lead discussions. However, large group presentations may be too impersonal. After a general presentation, peer facilitators as small group leaders can encourage students to think about the information, ask more questions, and seek knowledgeable people when they need help.

Sometimes issues related to sexuality are incorporated into courses such as life management skills, home economics, physical education, health education, and so forth. In this case, a trained peer facilitator may not be the leader of a discussion but, by example and timely use of interpersonal skills, can help make a discussion more meaningful.

Activity 15.1
The Ideal Mate

Purpose:

To examine characteristics that are related to selecting an ideal partner or lifetime companion.

Materials:

Paper and pencil; set of 12 traits (cards); scissors

Procedures:

1. Divide a piece of paper into 12 equal parts or squares. Number the squares from 1 - 12.

2. Divide a second piece of paper into 12 equal parts (cards) which are smaller than the squares in size. On each card write one of the following traits before cutting them out. Then, cut them out.

   1. Intelligent
   2. Attractive
   3. Good Conversationalist
   4. Shares Same Religious Values
   5. Athletic
   6. Ambitious
   7. Caring and Sensitive
   8. Status and Prestige in Community
   9. Interested in Same Activities
   10. Exciting and Fun to be With
   11. Good Sense of Humor
   12. Interested in Being a Parent

3. Randomly shuffle the cards. Take the first card from your stack and decide which square it should be placed on the numbered sheet of paper. If you place it on number 1, then you have ranked it the most important of all the 12 traits in choosing an ideal mate. If you place it on number 12, it is the least important of these traits to you.

Robert D. Myrick and Betsy E. Folk

4. Take the second card from the stack and place it on the numbered paper. You can move cards from one square to another, but only one card can occupy a numbered square.

5. Continue placing the trait cards until all 12 are placed in order of your priority, 1-12.

Key Questions:

Are there any other traits which you would have included for choosing an ideal mate? How would you discover whether someone has one of the traits you most value? In what ways are your top three choices like you and not like you? How does your ranking of the traits compare to your best friend's choices? Your parents' choices?

Activity 15.2
The Opposite Sex

Purpose:
To practice listening, clarifying, and responding to feelings. To learn more about the thoughts and feelings of the opposite sex.

Materials:
None

Procedures:

1. Form two circles of chairs—one inside the other (fishbowl).

2. The activity begins with all the boys in the class sitting in the inside circle, while all the girls sit in the outside circle.

3. As the girls listen attentively (no comments or clues about their reactions), the boys talk about:

   A. What do you think it would be like to be a girl?

   B. What are the advantages and disadvantages?

   C. What special problems and issues do girls face?

4. After eight to ten minutes, the boys stop talking. The girls then make the following responses related directly to what the boys have said.

   - 4 Clarifying or Summarizing Responses
   - 4 Feeling-focused Responses
   - 2 Open-ended Questions

5. Now, change places. The girls sit in the inside circle while the boys sit on the outside.

6. The same procedures as above are repeated. But, this time the boys listen (without comment) while the girls talk about what it would be like to be a boy.

7. After eight to ten minutes, the girls stop talking and the boys respond with a similar number of facilitative responses.

8. Next, the class sits in a large circle, arranged boy, girl, boy, girl....

9. Use the remaining time for a discussion about the activity, what was learned, what was relearned. Talk about the misconceptions.

Key Questions

What feelings and thoughts did you have as you listened? What questions would you like to ask a person of the opposite sex in order to gain more understanding?

Robert D. Myrick and Betsy E. Folk

Chapter 16

The Prevention of Career Indecision

You are close to making one of the most important decisions in your life. It is facing you and your classmates, whether you like it or not. You can make this decision without giving it much thought, or you can worry and fret about what to do, or you can plan for it. It is going to help determine your lifestyle, many of the people you meet, friends you have, some of your leisure activities, and even your own opinions about yourself. You are about to enter the world of work and to make a decision about jobs and careers.

All students eventually leave school. Some leave earlier than others. Some want to extend their education and continue on to colleges and universities or technical schools. Others want to gain more education and experience through military service. Still others want to get a job and start making money as soon as possible.

Choosing a career is not easy. Currently, there are over 20,000 different careers in the United States. New jobs are being created in order to keep pace with a fast changing world. Some jobs change or disappear altogether. There are more opportunities, especially for women, than there were a few decades ago. With so many possibilities, there is more pressure on young people to make the right choices, to pick the right jobs, to go to the right schools, and to discover the right careers for themselves.

Choosing a Career

A career might be described as a sequence of jobs which individuals hold in their working lives. There is a work history, usually a pattern of occupations or jobs which are related to a certain area or field of work. Unlike a career, a job does not necessarily extend over a period of time and is simply the assigned work duties and tasks a person may have when employed.

When you daydream about your future, do you think about the kind of work you will do? Do you have a picture of what a typical work day might be like? After all, more than half of most adults' waking hours are spent involved in work and earning money to support themselves. In general, your lifestyle centers around family, friends, leisure activities, personal development and well-being, and career. What do you see in your future?

There seems to be some evidence that those who are most satisfied with life, with their careers and jobs, are those who had a plan and followed it. Do you want to pick a job that best fits your interests, needs, and desired lifestyle? Or, do you intend to let chance determine your career and primary style of life?

Entering the World of Work

Of those students currently in high school, about half will go on to a college or university to gain more academic knowledge, which is needed in some highly technical or skilled jobs. About a third of those will drop out before graduating with a degree.

In general, men will be gainfully employed for about 40 years and most of this work will be outside the home in a work place. Traditionally, men have been cast in the role of primary provider for the family, while women have been seen as homemakers and part-time wage earners. But, this national scene has been changing.

Young women are entering the world of work earlier and staying longer. There are more opportunities for women in careers which were once considered "a man's job." This has encouraged many women to emphasize career development. Moreover, many are marrying later than their parents did. Some women are choosing not to marry at all. If they do marry, child bearing may be postponed while they establish their careers. Many leave their jobs for a brief period when their children are born, only to return later. In addition, there are many women who have no choice as to whether to work or not. They must provide for themselves and, in many cases, their children.

In 1990 almost half of all employed workers in the nation were women. While they work for many of the same reasons as men—to earn money, to be with other people, to have a feeling of accomplishment, and to add to their self-esteem—the biggest reason for working may be because of the high cost of living. Some families want a standard of living that requires two incomes to purchase the goods and services that they want. Dual career marriages are accepted and many times expected in families.

Joanne graduated from high school when she was eighteen and began work as a clerical assistant in a business firm. She worked there for four years, where she was promoted to a Secretary I position. She met new friends at work and during after work hours she socialized with some of them. It was at the firm where she met her future husband, Eric. They later married and had a child when she was twenty-six. Joanne wanted to stay home with the baby, but Eric's income was not enough to cover their living expenses. Returning to work seemed like the only option at the time. Joanne found a part-time job as a typist while the baby was in child care. When her second child was born, Eric was making more money, but expenses had also increased. Nevertheless, they decided to cut back on some things so that Joanne could quit her part-time job and go to community college where she started her studies in bookkeeping and accounting. By the time her children were in school, Joanne had entered the world of work again, but with a new career in mind.

Making Decisions About Careers

School is not easy for those students who find no meaning in it. They are unable to relate what they are learning to a job. Admittedly, there are many things taught in school which are designed to enhance a person's general education and general lifestyle. The mind of a person is a marvelous instrument which can provide a great deal of personal and social satisfaction when trained and stimulated. But, that may not be very appealing to a young person who lacks maturity, who is caught up with the events of a teenager's life, and who prefers specific job-related training.

Career awareness is becoming more and more important. Some students have very little information about the kind of jobs available and do not know how to plan for jobs or careers. Efforts have been made in many schools to expand student knowledge of jobs and explore work related skills. Yet, there is still a great need to increase awareness of the kind of jobs available, the skills needed to be successful, and of how jobs are related to personal identity, social fulfillment, and lifestyle.

For example, John grew up in a family of woodsmen in Oregon. He knew a lot about the logging business, including how trees were sawed and trimmed into cut-lengths of boards which were sold to lumber yards, who in turn sold them to the public. John's father was a "trimmer" in a mill where he operated a large band saw which cut the bark off a water-laden log fed in from a holding pond. He made several cuts so that large pieces of lumber fell on a chain. John's uncle was the "ratchet setter" who ran the equipment which flipped and turned the trimmed logs so the trimmer could make the best cuts. John's older brother worked on an outdoor platform called the "green chain." As the cut lumber passed his position, he pulled and rolled the big, heavy and wet pieces off the chain into a stack on some wooden "catch bunks," which were later taken away by a tractor-like carrier to a dry kiln.

John was hoping to get a job on the green chain after he graduated from high school. It paid good money for a job that required mostly hard labor. It also made it possible for him to learn about and move up to other mill jobs. John lived in a community where growing and cutting trees was the primary source of making a living. People talked about little else when it came to work. There were executives and sales representatives who sold the lumber to wholesale buyers, but John knew very little about their work since most of his knowledge about jobs came from being around family members. His family had been in the lumber business for decades and he expected to follow in their steps.

John's cousin, Scott, had made a decision not to work in a lumber mill. He knew that the community was already suffering economically as many of the big trees in the area had been cut. The future for the community looked bleak if it depended only on lumber. He knew that the computer industry was growing rapidly and that the demand for computer professionals would probably remain high for many years to come. Moreover, knowledge of computers could be applied in several fields and this increased the potential for employment. John's career goal seemed to require little thought; whereas, Scott needed more education and a plan.

Careers and Self-Identity

In the United States, work choice and work adjustment are almost always related to some kind of interpersonal skill. There is a personal investment which is reflected through self-understanding, values, goals, and personal traits. Energy levels, special interests, desired lifestyles, and personal ambition affect choices, willingness to work, and success.

Obviously, we would like to have jobs which pay well and add to our self-esteem. The kinds of satisfaction that we get from a job or working with others in a job setting are important and, subsequently, it is impossible to weigh these considerations in terms of money or social status alone. Ideally, we want a job which meets all our needs. But, there are almost always some compromises.

For example, a medical doctor is paid well for services provided to others. However, this profession requires many years of study and preparation and then many working hours. Doctors may be at a hospital with their patients before 7:00 in the morning and work on their records until after 7:00 at night. Would you be willing to spend this amount of time in a job?

Survival Skills in the World of Work

Employability skills are basic skills required in most jobs, such as being able to read, write, and apply simple math skills. These are taught in school. Yet, many employers report their primary concern is the attitude which young people bring to a job. If they are eager to learn, can follow directions, are punctual and reliable on the job, then their services will be valuable. If, on the other hand, they do not show up to work on time, are poor listeners, cannot accept criticism, and put forth only limited efforts, then they are likely to be dismissed or fired.

Schools attempt to provide students with employability skills. Every student before age eighteen should have the following:

- Knowledge of your personal strengths and weaknesses, preferences, values, and the ability to relate these to occupational choices and options. Making realistic self-estimates is an essential ability.

- Ability to explore and study existing job resources and educational opportunities.

- Ability to make decisions and solve problems in a rationale and purposeful way.

- Skills in interpersonal relationships, so that you can work cooperatively with others, understand and develop positive worker-supervisor relations, and adjust to different persons and job conditions.

- Knowledge of how to organize time and energy in order to complete a task and get a job done. This involves setting priorities and a willingness to follow through.

- Awareness of the changing world of work and how both job opportunities, the economy, and personal lifestyles and interests are related.

Learning About the World of Work

You can learn about the world of work through current publications and materials. For instance, eight of the 25 fastest growing jobs in the 1990s will be in health-related professions. Those specializing in environmental areas, such as toxic waste, and those who have an understanding of foreign trade will have an edge on many others. European markets will open many new opportunities for American workers.

Many teenagers learn about the world of work through their part-time and summer jobs while they are going to school. You might find a part-time job in a career area which interests you. This could give you opportunities to observe professionals or more experienced workers in the jobs and learn more about the work habits needed. Working part-time also allows you to try out some different jobs and become familiar with working environments.

A school work experience program can help students in career development. These programs combine academic studies in regular classrooms with on-the-job training and work experience. They may be called cooperative education, work study, or some other name.

Another way to gain experience is through volunteer work. For example, Ashley volunteered to work at an animal hospital because she wanted to gain more experience in working with animals. She was interested in becoming a veterinarian.

Robert D. Myrick and Betsy E. Folk

It is also possible to work on your own, especially if you have some special skills or interests. For instance, washing cars, painting houses, lawn care, and child care offer interesting opportunities typical for teenagers.

Peervention—
What Peers Can Do

Peer facilitators can help organize a career bulletin board, perhaps listing jobs in the community where students might be employed. The board might stimulate students to think about new jobs or those that are being replaced by new technology.

Tutoring students in employability skills is another valuable project. There are students who need practice operating a cash register, driving a truck, using a computer, or other work skills. Skilled peer facilitators can work as special tutors. They can assist people to get work permits, file for social security cards, and complete job application forms.

As special friends and small group leaders, peer helpers can work in projects where students practice writing letters of application or participate in "mock" interviews. They practice answering questions and learn ways in which to sell themselves to employers.

One project might be a peer-led set of activities in which students explore the kinds of jobs they would like to have, including whether the jobs are primarily focused on data, people, things, or ideas. Talk of what employers look for and the importance of first impressions when applying for a job can be interesting. A list of employer expectations might be discussed, as well as the kind of working conditions an employee might expect.

In one instance peer helpers provided a role playing activity in which students explored ways to get along with co-workers and what to do when there was a conflict on a job. Because self-understanding is so important to getting and keeping a good job, activities were also used which helped participants think about their self-concepts, goals, dreams, and career preferences.

School counselors, occupational specialists, and teachers appreciate peer helper assistance when they give and interpret aptitude tests and personality inventories. The counselors and teachers administer the measures, but peers can help people talk about the results. For example, one counselor used five peer helpers to work with 30 high school juniors who were undecided about their plans following graduation. General information was given to all the students in a large group. Then, each peer helper facilitated activities and group discussion with six students in a small group. Questions were posed, written down, and themes were summarized. Some of the questions were later addressed by the counselors when everyone met in a large group.

A group of peer helpers might work with a librarian or media specialist to construct a center in the school where students can research careers. For example, job centers were constructed in one school where students had opportunities to read about and take part in brief activities designed to help them learn more about the work performed in a job, the preparation and entry level procedures, and some of the advantages and limitations. Some career clusters were identified for the different centers, such as arts and humanities, business and office, communications and media, construction, health and hospital, recreation, marketing, and public service.

Peer helpers could help organize a series of guest speakers at the school, people who might talk about their careers and the path which led them to their positions. Field trips and on-site visitations might also be arranged. Films, film strips, and video tapes could be used. All of these, of course, are more meaningful when participants have an opportunity to talk with someone about what they experienced. Peer helpers would facilitate discussions and be prepared to refer students to other people and resources.

Six high school peer helpers went to an elementary school and worked with a class of fourth graders. They first organized the class into pairs of students, with one being a supervisor and the other the supervisee. The supervisees worked on their own and then began receiving criticism and suggestions from the supervising students. Sometimes the directions were harsh and critical and at other times they were more encouraging. Later, the class talked about the different ways people can be helpful when making suggestions and ways which seem to make things worse. Working in small groups, the peer helpers encouraged the fourth graders to think about whether they preferred direct or indirect supervision and they talked about jobs which required close supervision and those which did not. It was a career awareness activity with some work related skills and expectations.

Five peer helpers worked with 30 tenth grade students in groups of six each. They were asked to discuss the following:

- If your best friend wanted to quit school at the end of the tenth grade, what would you do?
- What reasons do people give for dropping out and what would you give for staying in school?
- How could you help?

Then, the students were asked to give themselves advice for getting the most out of school:

- What would you say to yourself?

General themes were identified, as well as specific actions needed to help get students in school.

These and other projects can be fun and productive. As you help others think about their futures, their potential careers, and what it takes to be successful in a job, you will learn too. You, too, will gain an increased understanding and appreciation of the choices you have in the world of work.

Robert D. Myrick and Betsy E. Folk

Activity 16.1
Remembering Career Choices

Purpose:

To increase awareness of how choices during high school affect future career opportunities.

Materials:

Paper and pencil

Procedures:

1. Choose one of your parents or a significant adult in your life to interview.
2. Using the following questions, interview the person and use your facilitative skills. Record their responses.

   a. When you were in high school, did you think about the job you wanted to have someday? What was the job? Did you get that job or did you change your plans?

   b. What is your job now and are you satisfied with it?

   c. If you could have another job instead of the one you have now, what would it be? Why?

   d. Looking back to your high school days, if you had it to do over, would you do anything differently?

   e. How did high school affect what has happened to you in your life?

3. After the interviews are completed, the class will discuss its findings.

Key Questions

What feelings and thoughts did you have as you listened? What did you learn? Did anything surprise you? How will the findings affect your decisions and choices regarding school and career?

Activity 16.2
Back to the Future

Purpose:

To increase career awareness regarding job clusters and to assess job opportunities in the future

Materials:

Paper and pencil. Career information sources (e.g. *Occupational Outlook Handbook*)

Procedures:

1. Divide a piece of paper into four columns. The four headings for the columns are: Data, Ideas, People, and Things. These are job cluster titles which describe what people primarily work with on the job.

2. Take one column at a time and list four or five occupations or job titles which fall in that category. For example, plumber might be placed under Things, while salesperson might be placed under People.

3. Examine your list and underline those which require a college education. Circle those where training on the job is all that is necessary.

4. Next, put an "!" after those jobs which you feel will be "hot jobs" in the future. Put a "?" by those you think are declining opportunities for the future.

5. As a class or in small groups, share your list with others.

6. Pair up with another classmate and research two of the jobs from your list, using the library or career information center.

Key Questions

What do you think the future holds for you, in terms of job opportunities? How will jobs change in the future? What factors will influence the change? How can you best prepare for the coming changes? What ideal job would you like to have someday? Under which column is it listed?

Chapter 17

The Prevention of Community Unrest

A recent nationwide study involved a series of interviews with more than three hundred adolescents. It investigated their thinking in terms of self, family, friends, attitudes toward work, and thoughts about the future. Interviewers went into many different homes, from the rich to the poor and from rural to inner city areas. It was concluded that no single factor contributes to the development of young people or the nation. Rather, it is the community, a combining of all the relationships in a person's life. And, it is the pattern of these associations within each community that determines our values, experiences, and future.

Every community is a complex pattern of relationships. It is difficult to describe its structure, although there are probably strong features which almost everyone recognizes. For example, one coastal community in Florida was settled decades ago by a large number of immigrants from Greece, who wanted to continue their heritage in the fishing and sponge industry. The community today is clearly marked by a Greek influence in such things as religion, food, and entertainment, but that is not all. Other nationalities have also impacted the area and will continue to do so for many years.

Likewise, farming communities in Nebraska are saturated with stories about the land and its crops. Young people in those communities know about farming equipment and the different words and phrases which describe the tilling of the land. They have their own unique way of life which has been shaped by the history, values, life styles, and relationship patterns in their community.

It is the same everywhere. All communities are unique. Yet, with mass communication being what it is today, almost every community is affected by radio, television, and VCR movies. Music Television (MTV) plays music designed for teenagers, as advertisers hope to cash in on the desires and interests of young people. Clothes designers, based in an urban area, determine the style of clothes which are manufactured and shipped to retail stores across the country. A shopping mall in one community will likely have many of the same items as that of a shopping mall thousands of miles away in a different state. The availability of all kinds of products set the stage for many of society's customs and styles.

Changing Communities

A few decades ago, life seemed to move at a slower pace. Life was less difficult. There were fewer choices, less stress, and fewer problems. Community unrest has increased over the past several years, threatening people's quality of life. This unrest is due to economic and social changes, all of which alter life styles and patterns of relationships in a community. Let us look at a few of the pressing issues in most communities.

Child care

The lack of available and affordable child care services has become a significant problem in our society. Quality child care is not a new issue, but it is becoming one of our nation's biggest problems.

A report from 77 cities across the nation showed that there is a crisis in child care. Overcrowded conditions, long waiting lists, growing numbers of latchkey and lock in children, inadequately trained and poorly paid child care providers accent the problem. There are simply not enough care givers.

In 1972, only twelve million mothers worked outside the home. Since that time, the number of married mothers in the workforce with infants under the age of one year has increased 108%. By 1995, it is estimated that two thirds of all preschool age children and nearly four out of five school age children will have a mother working outside the home.

For a great majority of families with two working parents, the second income is necessary to meet basic family needs—food, clothing, shelter, and transportation. In 1987, a congressional committee reported that 35% more two-parent families would slip into poverty if the wives were not employed. It is estimated that one out of five children live in poverty, and the number is even greater (one out of two) for some ethnic minority groups.

In addition, the nation is also filled with families who are headed by single parents. Currently, about 25% of the nation's children under eighteen years of age live in a one-parent home, which is typically headed by a woman victimized by poverty. It is this threat of poverty which jerks mothers out of their homes into the job market. In the meantime, the children must often tend to themselves, surviving on the help of their relatives, peers, and schools.

Although some employers are beginning to see child care assistance as a good investment for their work force, less than 3000 out of six million employers give employees any kind of child care assistance. Fortunately, there are a growing number of community organizations and agencies which are concerned about the problem. Many are banding together (e.g. The Alliance for Better Child Care) to help those who are finding problems arranging for child care. There is also an effort to gain more public support, including federal and state legislation.

Too many parents and children are in a bind and remain on welfare because there is no child care assistance. Too many children are coming home to empty houses and too many parents go to work worried about their children.

Latchkey kids

Who are the latchkey kids? They are children who care for themselves after school. The name comes from a child wearing the key to a house on a necklace. Nobody is quite sure of their numbers, but according to some estimates there are as many as 15 million such children who are unsupervised when they return from school.

The popular belief is that such children come from poor, single-parent families, living in high risk, inner city areas. However, research suggests that most latchkey children are from well educated, middle to upper class families living in suburban or rural areas. In these cases, self-care is a choice rather than a necessity.

Bigotry and troubling gangs

In 1964, the Civil Rights Act was passed. It guaranteed the rights of all Americans, emphasizing the value of diversity and cultural uniqueness. Now, years later, there is a disturbing resurgence of prejudice and bigotry. It takes many forms—from casual racial slurs at school to racist graffiti on lockers. It leaps out in disputes over symbols, flags, language, and territorial claims often turning into ugly confrontations.

Very few, if any, geographic areas or social settings seem to be immune from racial tensions. Incidents have been reported in rural communities as well as large urban districts, integrated schools as well as those that remain essentially segregated, and in the North as well as the South.

Many communities and states have changed in terms of the makeup of their populations. For instance, the majority of public school students in California are now members of minority groups. State department enrollment figures show that Hispanics, African-Americans, , Asians, and other minorities now make up an estimated 50.8% of the 4.6 million students enrolled in California schools.

Some people react negatively to anything that is viewed as special treatment for minorities, confusing fair representation and due process with personal rejection. The Skinheads and the Klu Klux Klan are visible groups which promote racism and anti-sematic beliefs. They have the right to voice their opinions even though their demonstrations and what they say are embarrassing to those who are educated. Some people worry that the rights given them by the constitution help legitimize their master race theories and myths. Their thinking must be challenged through debates and through legal procedures, rather than looking the other way.

Some gangs who are involved in illegal activities often attract teenagers who are considered "outcasts" by their peers. Gang members pride themselves for being different and unique. They are usually searching for their niche and trying to fit it, and most have not found it anywhere else. One critic said, "These are children of the "Me Generation" who have been taught that it is okay to be selfish, to be out only for yourself, and to do what you can to get a piece of the pie." But, they begin to fear that someone, or some group of people, is keeping them from getting what they want and deserve. Attempts to get rid of the competition or trying to get ahead by finding fault with others is the bigot's classic approach.

There are less visible forms of bigotry which are just as insidious. Racial violence has been promoted by some heavy metal rock music which features "white power" lyrics. Other song lyrics have messages of hate and violence against others.

The 1990s will be marked by many efforts to promote multi-cultural understanding. If successful, then community violence will be avoided and there will be more opportunities for people of different nationalities, races, and gender. There is a richness of heritage which can result from positive interactions among groups and this does not mean that unique cultural differences must be sacrificed. To the contrary, the positive differences are valued and respected.

Peer facilitators can assist others to talk and share ideas. They can participate in projects which encourage an understanding and appreciation of history, individual differences, and cultural values. They can work in projects which address community issues and which confront bigotry.

Peer facilitators can also make sure that they are not compromising their own beliefs and subtly supporting racist behavior. Many people, although well intended, are unaware of the roots of their own beliefs and behaviors. Peer helpers study themselves as well as others.

Increasing crime and violence

Within the past ten years, the number of juvenile offenders who have been sentenced from criminal activities has doubled in number. Ironically, these increases come at a time when the actual number of teenagers is decreasing compared to other age groups.

Two factors help explain the growing numbers. First, serious crime among young people has been fueled by a steady stream of drugs and weapons in the hands of offenders who are alienated from society. They do not see themselves as fitting in, or as part of a community.

They are hostile toward others, and they think only of their immediate needs and gratification. They have no goals or vision for the future. Second, this alienation is beginning early in life. Studies show that youths at risk can be identified as early as the second or third grade, when they began failing at school.

Simply waiting for "problem children" to outgrow their negative attitudes and behavior is a mistake. In most cases, they do not. They gain too much satisfaction of feeling powerful and in control of their lives by inflicting hurt on others. They destroy many of their opportunities in life but satisfy their drive to be recognized, even if it involves criminal behavior and correctional institutions.

The patterns of violent behavior can begin early in schools. One fourth grader, scared of some older youth, refused to go to school. He complained, "I don't feel good and have a stomach ache." A seventh grade boy had developed a pattern of truancy, poor grades, and signs of being a loner. A high school boy left home everyday with enough money to buy lunch, but usually went through the day without eating. In all of these cases, the students were being intimidated, robbed, or being forced against their will by bullies.

Fear of other students is said to be the reason that one out of every twelve students reports for dropping out of school. They do not see the school as a safe place to be. School officials may not be aware of the problem of violence or bullying in a school and parents may dismiss a child's concern with quick instructions such as, "Well, just tell your teacher, if it happens again."

Peer facilitators are not expected to confront bullies or criminals. They are not involved in school discipline, enforcing policies or procedures. However, peer helpers can be a safe harbor for those being victimized to explore the problem and think of what can be done next. In some cases, the peer facilitator will go with the student who is being harassed to a responsible adult. Then, in the presence of that adult, support the student's courage to report an incident or difficult situation.

States and communities need to invest more money and time into delinquency prevention programs. Such programs usually cost less and provide a greater return on the investment than waiting to catch and incarcerate a law breaker. However, many adults are unsure what to do. Peers can help think of ways of reaching young children, perhaps being a mentor to them, tutoring them, or helping them to get to school. Correcting the problem after the crime is a waste of time and energy. New alternatives are needed to help prevent crime for the sake of a safer and more productive community.

Peervention— What Peers Can Do

One peer group in a large urban city decided to help teach children to "Say No To Guns." They were influenced by Yolanda, a third grader, and her story: "I was taking a nap and I felt something hard under the mattress. I looked and it was a big ol' gun. I picked it up and wondered if it was loaded. Then, I threw it on the floor and ran away."

The Dade County School Board in Miami, Florida, was alarmed when it was reported that 40 children were killed by guns in 1989. The Board decided to develop a school program, the first of its kind, to promote gun safety in the schools, including an awareness day.

Peer facilitators can develop short skits which emphasize gun safety and what to do when a gun is discovered. The children play the roles of parents, police, and the youngsters who find a gun. They learn never to pick it up and, if they find one, to tell a parent or other adult. In one role play, a child suddenly discovers a gun and plays with it, mistaking it for a toy. Then, a child is shot. In the discussion which follows, students explore consequences, reactions, and rules of safety.

Teen's Talk Phone was started in Winter Park, Florida. The peer helpers completed a 40-hour training course and were available to talk to other teens about school, parents, friends, alcohol and drugs, or depression.

Ernest Boyer, President of the Carnegie Foundation for the Advancement of Teaching, after an extensive study about high schools concluded: "Teenagers can go through twelve years of formal education without becoming socially engaged, without spending time with older people who may be lonely, helping a child who has not learned to read, cleaning up the litter on the street, or even rendering some useful service to the school itself. And this life of detachment occurs at the very time students are deciding who they are and where they fit it."

Of course, there are notable exceptions to this profile and one of them is the work of peer facilitators who have chosen to take part in a community-focused helping project. Community service projects also provide a certain amount of job readiness skills, such as the experience of working cooperatively with others in a job setting and putting ideas learned in school into practice. The experience goes beyond mere textbook readings and is more relevant because it is related to real life. Peer facilitator clubs could organize programs based on the California Conservation Corps, which is the oldest, largest, and most successful state-run public service youth corps in the nation. The CCC fosters both conservation and youth development. It fights fires and floods, builds parks, cleans up environmental sensitive areas, installs solar heating systems in government buildings, and helps the forestry service.

There are numerous areas in the community where volunteer service would be a significant civic contribution. For instance, there are many older adults who cannot read and would benefit from tutoring. Hospitals and nursing homes appreciate the services of volunteers. Outpatients and elderly citizens who need care at home would value visits. Libraries, museums, and other public facilities can use volunteer assistance.

One community recognized young volunteers for their particular contributions in an annual ceremony. Among the winners of awards were those who volunteered time in law enforcement (police department), Girl Scouts, library reading program (Authors in the Park), playground supervision for mentally disabled children (bureau of parks and recreation), hospitals, city band and orchestra, a homeless shelter (Cold Night Program), Students Against Drunk Driving, and a city's Special Olympics for retarded children.

President Bush has encouraged volunteerism, especially in community service projects. He believes that school-based service efforts reaffirm the responsibilities of citizenship and the value of helping others. Senator Edward Kennedy has also stressed the importance of school-based approaches and said, "The 1990s can be the decade when we rediscover the importance of giving something back to the country."

Peer facilitators can become part of what President Bush called "1,000 Points of Light." As a peer facilitator, you can help light up someone else's world and in the process shed a brighter light on your own. Let your helping skills shine and help make the world a more gentle and kinder place to live.

Activity 17.1
Like Me and Not Like Me

Purpose:

To identify population groups which are "Like Me" and "Not Like Me" in order to explore attitudes toward people who seem to be different.

Materials:

Magazines, newspapers, scissors, glue, construction paper for a montage

Procedures:

1. Skim through the materials on hand and look for pictures which depict people who appear *different* from you. Cut them out.

2. Look for pictures which depict people who appear to be *like* you. Cut them out.

3. Divide your construction paper into two parts. One labeled "Like Me" and the other half labeled "Not Like Me." Leave some space between the two halves.

4. Make a montage using the pictures you have selected, placing them on the appropriate side of the paper.

5. Share your montage with others in the class.

6. In a class discussion, explore how the people in the "Like Me" side of the montage are different/similar from the people on the "Not Like Me" side.

Key Questions

How does it feel to be different from someone else? What does it feel like to be in the minority? Majority? What can be done to help minority and majority groups better understand each other? What barriers get in the way of bridging the gap between people who are different from one another? How is the class discussion related to current issues in the community?

Robert D. Myrick and Betsy E. Folk

Activity 17.2
The Community Machine

Purpose:
To demonstrate how different parts of a community can work together in harmony

Materials:
None

Procedures:
1. The class is divided into three groups of about five students each.

2. Each group member selects one of the following "community career sub-groups" to represent the behaviors, words, sounds, and/or movements which characterize the sub group. Ask yourself, "What can I do to show something about this group of workers?"

Community Career Sub-Groups

- Politicians
- Teachers
- Police Officers
- Carpenters
- Electricians
- Plumbers
- Doctors
- Truck Drivers
- Computer Specialists

- Judges
- Factory Workers
- Photographers
- Musicians
- Secretaries
- Cooks
- Elevator operators
- Bankers

3. Each group of students takes a turn forming a "Community Machine" with all its unique movements and sounds based on the career sub groups which were selected. One person begins and then a second joins in. Then, a third joins the machine until all five members of the group have become a harmonious machine.

4. After all groups have taken their turns, the class discusses the activity and their experiences.

Key Questions

How did it feel to be different from the others? Do you think the different sounds and movements contributed to your group's machine working harmoniously? What was needed to make it more harmonious? What might have happened if the career sub groups had been replaced by such sub groups as: race, religion, age, nationality, and different cultures? How are the class community machines like the real community in terms of working together yet being unique and different?

Code of Ethics*
for Peer Helpers

National Peer Helpers Association

June, 1990

Peer Helpers shall be people of personal integrity. As a minimum, the NPHA believes the peer helpers Code of Ethics shall contain the following and be evidenced by a commitment to and pursuit of:

1. A philosophy which upholds peer helping as an effective way to address the needs and conditions of people.

2. The individual's right to dignity, self-development, and self-direction.

3. Supervision and support from professional staff while involved in the program.

4. The development of a nurturing personality which:

   - Reflects a positive role model and healthy lifestyle (i.e., development and observation of a set of norms which guide behavior while in the program).

   - Rejects the pursuit of personal power, elitist status, or gain at the expense of others.

   - Strives to exemplify the peer helping philosophy in all life situations.

5. Maintenance of confidentiality of information imparted during the course of program-related activities. While confidentiality is the norm, certain exceptions shall be referred immediately to the professional staff. These exceptions include the following:

   - Situations involving real or potential danger to the safety or well-being of the peer helper, helpee, or others.

   - Child abuse, sexual abuse, and other situations involving legal requirements of disclosure.

   - Severe family dysfunction, psychotic behavior, extreme drug or alcohol abuse, and any other problems beyond the experience and expertise of the peer helper.

6. Personal Safety. Peer helpers must recognize, report, and know techniques to deal with potential threats to their emotional or physical well-being.

---

* A code of ethics is an agreement among those who commit to the program as to the norms which shall guide their behavior during their involvement in the program.

References

Bowman, R.P. (1986). Peer facilitator programs for middle graders: Students helping each other grow up. *School Counselor, 33*(3), 221-229.

Bowman, R. (1982). A student facilitator program: 5th graders helping primary grade problem behavior students. Unpublished dissertation. University of Florida, Gainesville, FL.

Bowman, R.P. & Myrick, R.D. (1987). Effects of an elementary school peer facilitator program on children with behavior problems. *School Counselor, 34* (5), 369-378.

Bowman, R.P. & Myrick, R.D. (1980). "I'm a junior counselor, having lots of fun." *School Counselor, 28*(1), 31-38.

Canning, J.H. (1985). *Play times: A structured developmental play program utilizing trained peer facilitators.* Minneapolis, MN: Educational Media Corporation.

Foster, E.S. (1983). *Tutoring: Learning by Helping.* Minneapolis, MN: Educational Media Corporation.

Kehayan, V.A. (1988). *Partners for change.* Ridgewood, NJ: Edu-Psych Outreach Center, Inc.

Myrick, R.D. (1987). *Developmental guidance and counseling: A practical approach.* Minneapolis, MN: Educational Media Corporation.

Myrick, R.D. & Bowman, R.P. (1981a). *Becoming a friendly helper: A handbook for student facilitators.* Minneapolis, MN: Educational Media Corporation.

Myrick, R.D. & Bowman, R.P. (1981b). *Children helping children: Teaching students to become friendly helpers.* Minneapolis, MN: Educational Media Corporation.

Myrick, R.D. & Erney, T. (1978, 1984). *Caring and sharing: Becoming a peer facilitator.* Minneapolis, MN: Educational Media Corporation.

Myrick, R.D. & Erney, T. (1979, 1985). *Youth helping youth: A handbook for training peer facilitators.* Minneapolis, MN: Educational Media Corporation.

Myrick, R.D. & Myrick, L.S. (1990). *The teacher advisor program.* Ann Arbor, MI: ERIC/CAPS.

Myrick, R.D. & Sorenson, D. (1988). *Peer Helping: A practical guide*. Minneapolis, MN: Educational Media Corporation.

Painter, C. (1989). *Friends helping friends: A manual for peer counselors*. Minneapolis, MN: Educational Media Corporation.

Painter, C. (1989). *Leading a friends helping friends program*. Minneapolis, MN: Educational Media Corporation.

Peterson, A.V., & Peppas, G.J. (1988). Trained peer helpers facilitate student adjustment in an overseas school. *School Counselor, 36*(1), 67-73.

Samuels, D. & Samuels, M. (1975). *The complete handbook of peer counseling*. Miami, FL: Fiesta Publishing.

Stone, J.D. & Keefauver, L. (1990). *Friend to friend: Helping your friends through problems*. Minneapolis, MN: Educational Media Corporation.

Sturkie, J. & Gibson, V. (1989). *The peer counselor's pocket book*. San Jose, CA: Resource Publications.

Tindall, J. (1989). *Peer counseling: An in-depth look at training peer helpers*. (Third edition). Muncie, IN: Accelerated Development.

Tindall, J.A. (1985). *Peer power: Becoming an effective peer helper, book 1, introductory program*. (Second edition.) Muncie, IN: Accelerated Development.

Tindall, J.A. (1989). *Peer power: Book 2, applying peer helper skills*. Muncie, IN: Accelerated Development.

Tindall, J.A. & Salmon-White, S. (1990). *Peers helping peers program for the preadolescent: Leader manual*. Muncie, IN: Accelerated Development.

Tindall, J.A. & Salmon-White, S. (1990). *Peers helping peers program for the preadolescent: Student workbook*. Muncie, IN: Accelerated Development.

Varenhorst, B.B. (1980). *Curriculum guide for student peer counseling training*. Portola Valley, CA: Peer Counseling.

Varenhorst, B. (1983). *Real friends: Becoming the friend you would like to have*. New York, NY: Harper Collins.

Robert D. Myrick and Betsy E. Folk